NEXT LEVEL TRIBE

How To Find, Connect & Keep
The People Who Matter Most

• • •

Jade Teta & Danny Coleman

Table of Contents

• • •

Introduction

• • •

By Jade Teta

I am at a networking event, a social gathering which during a subtler time would have been called a cocktail party. I have a love-hate relationship with these things. I hate them because I am an introvert, but not the typical introvert who gets social anxiety and hides in the corner. I am the oddball introvert who has zero social anxiety, but prefers to hang close to the wall, sip on a drink, and observe. That's the part I love: the people watching.

Some people are like magnets, attracting everyone around them. I love when these types first walk into the room; it's as if someone turns up the lights. Everyone notices them. It's not their fancy clothes, expensive jewelry or good looks people are responding to; it is something else. They are warm without being fake. They are present without being awkward or over-bearing. They are powerful in an inspiring, humble way. They are authentic, at ease, and they seem to make others feel the same way.

Then, there are those who seem to be wearing the human

equivalent of mosquito repellent. The ones who walk into a group and people scatter. Their smiles do not seem genuine. Their laughs are a little too frequent and a little too loud. Something just feels slightly off about them. They seem a bit too eager, too distracted or a little too indifferent. Maybe they are nervous, or maybe they are putting on a show; either way, people seem to want to move away from their energy.

There are the people who are talking too much, and those who are listening or pretending to listen. There are the couples, standing apart from the group, who you sense have just made a romantic connection. Some people are loud—obnoxious and over-the-top—others are soft spoken—forcing their conversational partners to lean in to hear their voices above the murmur in the crowded room. Some dress sharply, and some are rolling with the casual look.

But my focus always wanders back to the two species of social animals I am most fascinated by: those everyone loves and wants to connect with, and those who everyone avoids. What is it about those unable to socialize that puts people off? Why can't they connect? And, how about the people that effortlessly charm others - the ones who, as they walk away from a group, leave everyone in their wake feeling enhanced and better about themselves.

If there is a singular truth about us humans, it's that we need social connection. Air, water, and food may feed our bodies, but social connection is the only thing that feeds our hearts. Why do some people feed us and others don't?

This thought has occupied my mind since I was a boy, people watching from the walls of my childhood. I was curious as to why some of my teachers were despised and others were loved. Why did kids pass notes and whisper about certain classmates and not others? What was different about the kids who were universally respected and revered, from those who barely registered? Even as a child, I knew social dynamics were impacting everything about us.

The answer came to me when I was in high school. I had a friend on my football team named Cleo—I love that dude and still think of him. He was black and I was white. I grew up in the South. Cleo and I played football together. We saw each other at school, but black and white kids did not normally hangout otherwise. The town we grew up in was somewhat segregated, and Cleo and I were from different neighborhoods. Back then most kids stayed on their side of the tracks. Except for Cleo, our friends, and me.

Cleo and all my other black friends were over at my parents' house all the time. I suppose I understood it was not the norm, but it never fully dawned on me until later.

One day, as Cleo was leaving, he said something to the effect of, "Man, I love it here. It feels like I am part of the family, like I am an Italian kid just like you." I don't remember exactly how he said it, but that sentiment has always stuck with me.

And he was right. My parents treated him and everyone else in my group of friends like they were part of the family no matter what. My friends became so comfortable that they would walk into the house, open the refrigerator and grab some OJ. My mom would come in and give them a kiss and a hug, just like they were her own kids.

My father was the same. He would come home from a long day of work, see all the kids—a smile spreading across his face—and ask them if they had eaten. Instead of hiding away from the clamor in a study or the garage like some work-weary parents did, he would put on a huge pot of his homemade tomato sauce and my army of high school friends and I would eat, talk shit, laugh and connect. Today, those "kids" are adults with children of their own. They still, on occasion, drop by my mother and father's house to say hello as a part of our ever-expanding, extended family.

My parents are Next Level connectors. They taught me at a young age how to feed people, not just with food, but with social, emotional and spiritual energy. It came easily to them—it wasn't forced. I never heard my parents complain about people. They were unconcerned with trivial, petty issues or gossip. They did not expend unnecessary energy stressing out about things they couldn't control or what other people were or were not doing. It was their natural way, and they were loved for it.

They are not unique either. I have known other people who are the same way. Displaying authentic kindness, these people have a caring curiosity, and an ability to make other people feel loved and appreciated.

It has always bothered me that these people aren't the ones who get the accolades. Instead, we talk about who has the largest social media following. We focus on commercial and media-driven success like book deals, successful CEOs and movie stars. We praise the people "crushing it"— whatever that means? We celebrate the guys making more money, more career gains, taking more tropical vacations, and buying the most expensive cars.

It's backward. So, you have thousands of social media followers and are posting overused motivational quotes about how you are "killing it?" Is that what our society calls success now? That's not how I define it.

To me, success is how you touch, move, and inspire the person right in front of you. When people interact with you, what are they left with? We have the power to make a difference for

4

others with a genuine smile and a hello. We can make some-one else's day by giving just a little bit of our time and pres-ence. We can alter a person's life in meaningful, powerful and positive ways with our kindness, generosity and humanity. The people who understand that and see it as part of their job on this planet; those are the most successful people in my opinion. They make a huge difference for us all, and they ask nothing in return.

Here is what I know for sure: We, humans, want to do some-thing of substance. We want to live meaningful lives that matter. That is what we crave. We want people to see us. We want ac-knowledgment. We want to be heard and be held. We want to be the guy or girl who lights up a room, and who people love and celebrate. We want people to pay attention and care about us.

That is normal; we would not be humans if we did not feel this drive. The problem is we often abandon humanity in the process of seeking it. At the end of your life do you think you are going to be remembered for your perfect six-pack or your wrinkle-free face?

Is anyone going to say, "Man, I am going to miss seeing Jade drive around in that Ferrari."? Or "Wow, remember how amazing Jade's trip to Maui was? I will never forget all the pic-tures he posted on social media." Or "Jade had money—I al-ways enjoyed seeing all the nice things he bought."

What people are going to remember about you is that you noticed them. How you connected and made them feel is what will stay with them once you are gone. They will think back to how you cared, and the times you showed up. They will be in-spired by what you left for others, not what you kept for yourself.

I have a tattoo on my back that says, *Relinquam Amor*. It's Latin for, "leave your love." I got it as a reminder of what is most important. To me there are three imperatives in life: to learn, to teach, and to love—the word "love" encompassing sharing as well. It is no coincidence that all three involve other people.

You can't fulfill any one of these imperatives by yourself. You need other people, and they need you to truly succeed. To make a meaningful difference in life, you have to connect. You have to engage. You must learn, teach, and love.

I am tired of always celebrating rich CEOs and risk-taking entrepreneurs. Don't get me wrong, I respect and value the visionaries who have unlocked technological advances that have revolutionized the world we live in and given us our amazing devices. But it is the individual connectors that provide life with its greatest joys. I want to further celebrate those connectors. The mothers and fathers. The teachers. The coaches. The cashier who makes everyone passing through his aisle feel welcome and warm. The barista who loves coffee, but loves people more. And all the people loving and connecting with their fellow humans.

For those who feel disconnected and distant, this is a book to help you understand how to get back to your roots; how to elevate yourself—and those around you—by using the Three R's: by being Real, by being Responsive, and by Recognizing the gifts and contributions of others. This is how to connect to what truly matters to you, and reconnect to your meaning and purpose in this life.

We humans are not islands unto ourselves. I often ask myself, "Jade, if you are not here to help, then why the hell are you here?" There is no more important work in the world. There is nothing more powerful than real connection.

Do you realize how many people you will be in contact with in a day who need you? They are lonely, lost, hurt, confused, and scared—hiding behind bland smiles and generic responses of "Fine," when you ask, "How are you?" in that meaningless way we all do as we go about our days. And you walk right by them. They walk past you in the grocery store. You are in their checkout line. They merge into traffic next to you. They walk their dog through your neighborhood. They read your social media posts.

Are you going to continue to look past them? Are you going to insist they take notice of you first? Or are you going to reach out and connect?

There is only one way to feel the connection and love you seek, and that is to invest it in others first.

This book gives you the tools to do just that.

A Next Level Friend

I just finished a workout. I had just flown back to my hometown in North Carolina from my residence in Santa Monica, California. I own a gym in North Carolina, and man, it was nice to be back. My two closest friends in the world are there, my older brother, Keoni, and our mutual best friend, Ronnie. We have not seen each other for almost a year, and they know I have some deep, emotional wounds I have been working through.

The workout is over. We are laughing and shooting the shit; reminiscing about old times. Ronnie intuitively knows the exact moment to check in, but he does not ask me how I am doing. He simply says, "Jade, you know we are here for you man. Don't be a freakin' chump."

I did not even have to say it; he knew. "Don't be a freakin' chump" is a Ronnieism. It means: I love you, I got you, you're not alone, you matter to me, and I am your family. I look at him and nod, and he knows I understand. Ronnie is part of my Tribe, that group of people who are my chosen family. The ones that are always there, and always care. I don't share any of my feelings with him just yet. I need a little more time. But Ronnie knew what I needed to hear, and he knew the right time, and the right way to say it.

The next day Ronnie texts me. He wants to go for a hike. I am still not ready to talk, and I tell him I have some things to do. I have not fully realized it yet, but he knows I need him. His text is a reminder. It is his way of saying, "Hey man, you are not getting off that easy. I know you've got something on your mind."

The next day we both arrive at the gym early. Ronnie walks up to me and gives me a hug. He says, "It's time bro, get me caught up." I look at him and tell him what he already knows; I am still in pain. He listens, in only the way certain people can.

That talk lasts almost three hours, and it is exactly what I need. It is the connection I had been craving. Had Ronnie not been interested or sensed it, I may have gotten sidetracked with other priorities; he knew me better than I knew myself. I am an open and emotionally available guy, and I am not one to hide my feelings, or try to suck it up. But, I am also not the type who talks a lot about my stuff to others. I make a living off of listening to others; I had gotten in a bad habit of not sharing a whole lot about myself.

You know that feeling you get when someone goes out of their way for you, but your intuition tells you they are going to hold it against you or expect something in return? I hate that feeling. I try to avoid this type of person at all cost. Because of this, I am very selective in who I trust and confide. I often wall myself off in a way that is not healthy, thinking I can handle it all myself.

Ronnie sees this in me. He does not call me out or patronize me. He does not judge me. He simply shows up for me in a way that helps me recognize this dysfunction in myself. He gave up his entire afternoon, missed an appointment, and did not look at his phone a single time during the entire conversation. He stayed present with me. He showed up for me again, like so many times before. This is why I trust and love him. I know through past experiences that I can count on him, that he has zero expectations of me, and no requirement of anything in return.

Some people are there for you without ever needing to be asked. You may not even realize you need them, but they realize it and act on it. You may wonder, "How did they know?" Those are the people you keep. Ronnie is one of those. He is a member of my Next Level Tribe.

The Three Human Levels

The way I see it, there are three types of people that live inside all of us: Base Level Human, Culture Level Human and Next Level Human.

This is not a judgment or a "better than" thing. That's why I call it "Next Level" and not "Higher Level."

Our Base Level selves are motivated by fear. It is our lizard-brain self. The part of us that feels like everyone is out to get us, the side of our personality that feels like it is us against the world. When we are operating from Base Level, we lie, we bullshit, we avoid, we attack, and we manipulate. We behave as if someone is trying to take something from us. We feel an overwhelming need to protect ourselves and fight back. When we are in Base Level, it is all about us, everyone else be damned. The Base Level operates by the mottos "Take what you can get," "Every man for himself," "Winner take all," and "An eye for an eye."

Culture Level is about status and standing. Our Culture Level self seeks a team to be a part of. You can think of this side of your personality as the section that has stayed stuck in high school. It is the adolescent you. This side gossips, judges and is two-faced. Culture Level deems some people as worthy, popular types, and others as losers or undesirables. When we are operating from Culture Level, there is an us versus them mentality. At this level, we feel jealousy, inadequacy, and a need to overcompensate or boast. Culture Level behavior involves trying to elevate our own status while lowering someone else's.

Next Level is about growth and connection. In fact, Next Level types don't seek competition; they seek collaboration. Our Next Level selves know that other humans are some of our greatest sources of meaning, they also realize other people grow us in ways we could never achieve alone. This is the part of our personality that feels connected to others through our common humanity. This side of ourselves wants other people to succeed, and we will sacrifice our own needs for the greater good. When we operate from our Next Level instincts, we recognize that helping others elevate does not hold us back, but rather helps us go Next Level too. Where Base Level and Culture Level are more self-centered, Next Level is more self-aware, self-actualizing and selfless. These types operate by what I call the "3 Imperatives:" to learn, to teach and to love. Their motto is, "We are all in this together," and they operate via the platinum rule: treat others, not how you want to be treated, but how they want to be treated.

The Next Level Tribe
Think about the people who make up your inner circle. Are they friends like Ronnie; Next Level types who support you,

want you to win, and are willing to sacrifice time, energy, and emotional resources for you? Are they in competition with you; Base Level types who seem to subtly undermine you with passive aggressive comments, shady behaviors and manipulative tendencies? Are they the Culture Level types; the kind of people who seem to be friends when it is convenient for them and you are behaving exactly how they want you to? I had a very close friend; let's call her Rebecca. Rebecca had a series of affairs, and went through a divorce. Since I was one of her closer friends at the time, I watched her go through some extremely painful situations.

She had an amazing life. She had good friends, so she thought. But when all of this went down, the judgment that she endured was horrifying to me. She lost friends, had family members turn on her, and found herself alone with not many people to trust.

I also lost friendships with people because I would not allow them to badmouth her around me. It seemed I was the only one coming to her defense. This was so destructive in so many ways, that Rebecca retreated from most everyone, including friends like me, who had her back.

When it feels like the entire world is against you, it is difficult to put faith in your Next Level self. I lost touch with Rebecca. She started to see me as the enemy. The Base Level hate, and the Culture Level judgment pushed her to retreat into her own Base Level behavior. She became paranoid and angry, and cut off communication. I had another friend, David. David went through a similar circumstance as Rebecca, except he was on the other side of things. His wife betrayed him. He was devastated, but his friends were Next Level types. They did not judge his wife or him. They did not abandon him or her. They helped him see the pain as an opportunity to grow, to learn and to get better. David leaned on his Next Level friends, taking their coaching and soaking up their counsel. In the two years of separation that ensued, he became a better, more loving person. He went Next Level too. He worked on himself, took responsibility for his part, and transformed to a more present and loving person. When the dust settled, he was better for having had the experience. He and his wife fell back in love, and their relationship is one built on trust and honest communication. You might judge Rebecca for her behavior. You might blame David's wife for hers. You may see perpetrators and victims in these stories. You would be acting in a normal, predictable way if you did. But you would also be acting from your Base Level or Culture Level personality. Maybe you remember a time you were betrayed, and hearing about Rebecca or David's wife triggers your Base Level Self? You remember the hurt, that hurt triggers your anger, and that anger gets projected onto these people.

If you were a Next Level Human and a Next Level Friend, you would see the situation for what it is; humans getting caught up in the messiness of being human. Of course, you would not condone the behavior, but you would have compassion. You would not let your own wounds be triggered, and you would not let your adolescent judgments take over. You would simply seek to be there for your friend, and make sure they seize the opportunity to grow and get better as a result.

This is what Danny and I mean by Next Level Tribe. These are the people who are there in your worst times. They are there again and again and again. They forgive you over and over.

They have your back. They make the time. Next Level Tribe members show up for you even when you don't show up for them and can't show up for yourself. They are the people who act as anchors and lighthouses in the storms of life. They are always available, no matter how much time has gone by or what was said. These are the types we all need. Their impact is so powerful they elevate you to your Next Level. Rebecca did not have those types around her. David did.

Psychology research tells us that there are three factors more important to your success in life than anything else; more important than IQ, social intelligence or emotional intelligence. They are:

1. the belief you have in yourself
2. the belief others have in you
3. the ability to turn stress, hurt, tragedy and pain into fuel for growth.

All three of these factors can be enhanced by other people. Next Level Friends and a Next Level Tribe are the critical components of living a healthy, happy meaningful life that makes a difference.

This book is about helping you learn how to be a Next Level Friend so you can build your Next Level Tribe.

PART 1

• • •

WHY CONNECT?

By Jade Teta & Danny Coleman

*"He alone has lost the art to live who
cannot win new friends."*
—S. Weir Mitchell—

Why Did We Write This Book?

• • •

From Jade......

I am feeling miserable. It has been two days and I can't shake what feels like immense sadness. What is happening to me? Is this what other people call depression?

At 35 I wasn't as familiar with depression as I am now. I mean, I had felt sadness and disappointment at times, but it was fleeting and I could eventually shake it off. I couldn't figure out why I was feeling so down.

I definitely had things to be sad about, I suppose. I was recently separated from my wife, who I loved, after I had an affair. I had to manage all the things that came along with that, and what happened when I told my wife—facing my own dishonesty, overwhelming emotions from all sides, anxiety, and all the rest. In the end, I opted to take some time alone.

That was a few years back and it had never really affected me all me too intensely until it hit me so hard it practically knocked me off my feet.

Aha. That was the answer. I had made the drive from North Carolina to California to rediscover myself and pick up the pieces. But instead of "finding myself," I had inadvertently isolated myself. In an effort to get back to focusing on me, I left my family, my friends, and my entire support system. I distanced myself from my Tribe, no wonder I was feeling so disconnected and depressed. I chuckled a bit when this realization hit me.

I remembered reading *Into the Wild*, the story of Christopher McCandless. If you've never read the book or seen the movie, it's a true account written by journalist Jon Krakauer about a young college graduate who disappears from his life without telling anyone. He drives across the United States from East to West coast until his car breaks down. He eventually hitchhikes his way through Canada to Alaska and heads off into the wilderness to live off the land.

He carries a journal and records his journey and thought processes. To him, society was the problem. He wanted to escape from it; too many people, too many considerations, too much, period. Soon he finds himself alone, isolated, and starving. He is unable to manage, and through a tragic set of circumstances, starves to death, alone in the Alaskan tundra. The last words inscribed in his journal were, "Happiness only real when shared."

His body was found months later.

So, here I am in my own self-imposed, isolated wilderness. Except my "wilderness" was Santa Monica, California. And I wasn't alone. Not if I didn't want to be.

I realized I was making some of the same mistakes as McCandless, believing that I could and should go it alone. I recognized I had hurt people close to me, people who trusted me. I had also placed my trust in someone who betrayed me, but I had not been a great friend either. This was a hard realization.

One of my favorite philosophers is Bruce Lee. He has a quote I love: "To know yourself, study yourself in action with others." This ordeal woke me up to a part of myself I did not like. And, although I was beginning to grow, I was also learning that growth can be uncomfortable.

Here I was, taking on the gargantuan task of rebuilding myself, and I was all alone. I knew enough through my training as a physician and my background in counseling and coaching that other people were not the problem; I was. But knowing you are to blame, and doing something about it are two different things. I had to take concrete action or this self-realization was going to become self-loathing.

With that in mind, I took two steps. First, I wrote out what I came to call an Honor Code. It started as a set of principles to which I would commit and hold myself accountable. It was a strange idea that came out of nowhere, but I needed an anchor. It felt like the best first step.

Next, I took action related to the principles I had chosen. I didn't sit around thinking positive thoughts or hope for a truckload of love and acceptance to appear at my door. I made moves.

Here is a line straight from my Honor Code: "Kindness will be my religion, honesty my practice and generosity my action."

That's where I started. I read that sentiment in my Honor Code aloud for several days. I let it settle into me. Then one day I walked out into Santa Monica. I withdrew the maximum of $200 from an ATM and had the cashier at a nearby gas station change the money into 1's, 5's, and 10's.

I proceeded to walk around Santa Monica giving money to random strangers. Some of them were homeless and some of them were not. Many of them talked to me. Some told me stories. Others asked me to tell mine.

I listened to the stories. I heard heavy and sad stories. I heard exciting and thrilling stories. I heard stories of happiness and love. I heard stories of loss and sorrow. I saw confident, capable people who inspired me. I saw broken, regretful types, who scared the shit out of me.

One man I met was sitting on a bench near the promenade. It was getting dark, and there were not many people around. He saw me and must have sensed I was coming to talk to him. He startled me when he said, "Son, sit down here; let me tell you something about life."

I sat down without saying a word. We had not even introduced ourselves. He said, "I have been through three marriages. One I lost to cancer, one I lost because I was stupid, and one I lost because she was stupid. You know what all that taught me?" "Two things," he said; "First, I can survive anything. Second, it is never too late to start over. I am 73 years old. I fought in Vietnam, and I can tell you those marriages were way tougher than that. I can also say they made me a better person."

That was it; that is all he said. He then handed me a penny and got up and walked away. Confused? So was I. This story seemed the perfect message for me at the perfect time. His story and his demeanor have stuck with me to this day. I don't know if he was homeless or not. I don't know why he gave me that penny and I don't know how he knew I was coming to talk to him. All I know is, it was the perfect story, the one I needed to hear to know that my pain was neither unique, nor special. This dude had been through way more.

I spent hours that day with people. I returned to my apartment and I couldn't remember the last time I felt that happy, grateful, and connected.

My "issues" seemed like nothing more than a stubbed toe

or a mosquito bite in the grand scheme of potential life hurts. What I was going through seemed trivial in the face of so much honesty. Through my interactions with others, I was able to generate a feeling of immense gratitude for my life. I was charged up by the energy others gave me.

Complete strangers provided the charge I needed because I decided to give it to them first. I required nothing in return. This was the beginning of my process: the realization that if I was to change and get better, I needed to build an elevated Tribe as well. That is where the genesis of this book came from. I had been in the health and fitness fields acting as a coach, counselor, mentor and trainer for close to thirty years. I had all the training and know-how and yet I missed the most essential requirement of every human on the planet; being part of a Tribe. We are powerful as individuals, but a Next Level Tribe makes us superhuman. That is why it is so important. But not just any Tribe will do. To become a Next Level Human, you need a Tribe of Next Level Humans.

From Danny ......

When I was getting ready to enter college, people in their 40's and 50's said it would be the greatest time of my life. It's "the perfect intersection of freedom and responsibility" they'd say. You're finally free of your parents' reign, but you don't have any bills or large life commitments yet. It's the only time where you are in an isolated bubble of other kids your age, where you can experiment and explore, free of judgment and with limited consequences.

That wasn't my college experience.

I didn't join a fraternity. I didn't take part in any clubs. I didn't make any lifelong friends. I went to four different colleges in five years. Every time I started making friends, I transferred to a new college or moved to a new city. Every experiment I ran, and avenue I explored, came with *a lot* of consequences and judgment. I went through my first major heartbreak and all of the emotional turmoil that comes with it. I worked more than I attended class, and hung out with people who were two to three times my age.

It was the opposite of the "best time of my life."

While most students were meeting and connecting with new people, I began building lifestyle habits that isolated me from others. I didn't spend my free time meeting up with friends, working on projects, or intermingling with dorm mates. I wasn't going to parties or participating in intramurals.

I watched television, read books, worked out alone with my headphones blaring rap music (the more profane the merrier), and ate more popcorn than any human being should eat (which definitely isn't socially sexy). Without noticing, I was slowly building a lifestyle of loneliness.

The more I unconsciously isolated myself, the less I *wanted* to connect and socialize. The momentum of my bad habits was taking hold. I'd screen calls from my closest friends and family members. I'd turn down invitations to go out with new people because "I was just going to relax tonight." It felt like a black hole I'd never escape.

And, with the pattern of hopping from school to school every year, I got to a place where I didn't even try to make new friends because I thought, "I won't be here long." It was textbook "learned helplessness" that all the psychology books I was reading talked about.

In high school, I had a huge circle of friends. I started on the basketball team and had an amazing home life with my mom and two brothers. Almost every moment of my day was spent surrounded by people. "Alone time" consisted of sleeping in on a Sunday morning.

In college, I spent 90% of my day alone.

What stuck with me most about my college experience wasn't The 4 P's of Marketing, or some party I attended. It was the realization that having a floundering social life can destroy a person's motivation, happiness, and energy.

But, this is where my extremely depressing story stops. I promise. I'm sorry I had to put you through that. From here on out, it's only good jokes and personal stories of how wonderful a dancer I am.

As much as reading about my college experience may have made you want to cut your right arm off with a butter knife, it was important to share. I learned the hard way that we are not islands unto ourselves. Other people are an essential ingredient in our lives. They impact everything from our health, to happiness, to our success at work.

I went from top of the world to bottom of the barrel, and it was exclusively because I went from having a Next Level Tribe to being a lone wolf. That is what we aim to teach you in this book. It's a guide on how you can consciously create a group of people who improve every area of your life.

A Call For Connection

Research shows that rejection and isolation activate the same regions of the brain as a physical pain, like getting punched in the face. In a study titled "Very Happy People," researchers sought out the characteristics of the happiest 10% among us. There was only one characteristic that separated the happiest people from the rest of us: social support.

In college I had slowly curated a world of isolation, and the pain that comes with it.

Not only do other people make us happier, but they make us better people ourselves.

Doctors who form stronger connections with their patients are rated as better physicians. Salespeople with a greater capacity for empathy sell more products. And people with fit friends are more likely to be fit themselves.

We all intuitively understand this on some level. It's better to drink with friends than to drink alone. We don't play pick-up basketball without others. We don't take ourselves on a dinner date. We know that social support, laughter, sex, shared experiences, and ordinary moments of connection are the memories we have on our deathbeds.

Yet, the way we live our lives does not align with this knowledge. Our new 24/7 society perpetuates isolation and loneliness. We have learned to value things like focus, productivity, promotions, likes, follows, look-at-me's, hustling until your face falls off, popcorn eating (Oh, just me?), and competition.

But this way of life isn't conducive to connection. It's a vicious cycle of blocking others out. Focus is done alone. Competition means I win, you lose. Look-at-me means forget-about-you.

Isolation is a subtle and slow process so we don't see it coming. We focus more at work, our bank accounts rise and our performance ratings soar, but we can't remember that last time we laughed with a loved one or played a game of hoops just for the sake of playing.

We collect "stuff," work harder to pay for that stuff, sleep less so we can work harder so we can get more of the "stuff," end up with less family time and more stress. And when we get stressed, our default response is to double-down and focus more. We isolate ourselves at our desks or the corner of the library, just like I did in college. Stress leads us to disengage from others, rather than move towards them. We're too busy to make time for frivolous activities like hanging out with friends or chitchatting with loved ones.

Ironically, the most powerful secret of success and happiness is our ability to connect and form relationships with others. When our relationships are thriving, we perform better at work, are presented with more opportunities, are less stressed, and perceive challenges as easier to overcome.

This is why Jade and I chose to write this book. We hate the social media society of follows and likes and the staged lives we all present online. We hate the idea of success as a zero-sum game—I win, you lose—the idea that money and accolades are what separate the winners from the losers.

This false sense of popularity and connection is leaving us all more isolated and lonely. This book is a manifesto to break this chain. It's a call to spend less time on your investment portfolio and more time on your social portfolio.

It's a call to stop all the bullshit, "influence tactics," and social skills that champion manipulation. It's a guide on how to surround yourself with people who make you better, happier, and healthier. It's a complete roadmap to build your Next Level Tribe.

PART 2

• • •

Social Agility: How To Connect With Your Next Level Tribe

By Danny Coleman

"Social relationships are the single greatest investment we can make when it comes to our happiness."
—Shawn Achor—

Connection & Being
Socially Agile

• • •

I n high school I played basketball. Every day after school we would run drill after drill. We would work on dribbling with our left hand, our right, and behind the back. We'd practice layups, free throws, and 3-pointers. We'd work on our defensive slides, our agility, and our rebounding.

We practiced the fundamentals until they were such deeply ingrained habits that I was setting picks at the mall and doing imaginary crossovers in my living room.

But when it came to the actual game, the drills no longer mattered. It didn't matter how much you practiced using your left hand if the defense continually forced you to go right. It didn't matter how good you were at boxing out if the rebound went the other direction.

This is the same reason most social skills, and relationship advice, frankly, sucks. Social Skills gurus give us a list of drills to practice, but if we don't understand the context of the game, we won't succeed.

When we're taught how to connect with others, we get advice like this: Smile. Shoulders back. Head up. Tight buns. Nod your head, but not too much. Eye contact, again, not too much. Shake their hand firmly, not too tight, but tight enough.

Okay, great, you checked all of the tactical boxes. You have phenomenal posture, but you forgot the other person's name, forgot what they said, and had way too much eye contact anyway. Or not enough.

And that's the problem. We are so focused on executing the drills that we miss the flow of the game. Practicing tactics, like practicing basketball drills, is helpful and an important part of the process. You should absolutely practice better posture when you're at your desk, practice eye contact in the mirror, and practice smiling more in the shower.

Recently in an interview I listened to with entrepreneur, Gary Vaynerchuk, he said, "I'm about religion, not tactics." He said, "The biggest truth and the best 'hack' is when you can speak to the religion of what your tactics are trying to accomplish—the big picture of what you want to make happen."

He's saying when you become a certain type of person; the tactics will naturally fall into place.

Winning basketball games is a lot like connecting with others. It has a lot to do with *context and character, and it's the first step in creating a Next Level Tribe.*

We call it becoming *Socially Agile*: the awareness and adaptability to form a connection with anybody. Social Agility isn't about more tactics and to-dos. It's the understanding of the flow of the game. It's less about tactics and strategies, and more about who you are. Social Agility is about having fun and playing the game. It's the religion of social skills and connection.

So many of us *want* to connect with other people. We crave

deep friendships, romantic relationships, and enriching conversations. We want to be chosen by others. We want to get invited to the gala, get promoted, strike up interesting conversations with strangers, and be bought a beer.

But we are misguided by traditional social skills advice and influence "methods." We lack the basic tools to connect with another human being. This is why the first step in building your Next Level Tribe is becoming Socially Agile. Once you learn how to connect with anybody, you get to choose who gets to be in your Tribe and who doesn't.

The 3R Model of

Becoming Socially Agile

• • •

L et's say you're a plus one at a wedding. You walk into the reception area after a lovely ceremony. You're standing tall, smiling wide. Love is in the air, why wouldn't you be? Everybody is cleaned up and dressed to the nines. The drinks are flowing. Everybody's looking good, feeling good.

You grab a few meatballs on a stick that are being carried around on shiny silver trays. Spotting the mother of the bride sitting at the table alone, you walk over and have a seat next to her. You thank her for those delicious meatballs on a stick. You charm and flatter her. You even make her laugh a few times.

A few moments later you're hanging out with the grandfather of the groom, listening as he tells you the story of his wedding and all the adventures he's had since.

You teach a nephew to do the Wobble, and a niece to do the Electric Slide. You shake hands. You crack jokes. People who were strangers an hour ago now feel like old friends.

This is Social Agility in action. It's the ability to authentically connect in any situation.

Social Agility has three components, what we call the Three R's of Social Agility.

Responsiveness: Paying attention to the world and people around you and having the awareness to adapt accordingly.

Recognition: Noticing and actively appreciating other people for who they are. Every person in the world has something interesting, valuable, or insightful about them and it's your job to find it.

Real: Showing up authentically in the world and attracting the right people into your Tribe.

You become Socially Agile when all three are working together.

If you're Responsive and practicing Recognition, but you're not Real, people will walk all over you, and you'll be seen as a pushover.

If you're Real and Responsive, that's great, but you'll appear cold.

Embodying Real and Recognition? That's a good start, but you'll come across as distant and in your own little world.

True social geniuses embody all three of these elements.

Responsiveness

"Another one of my most common pieces of advice is that it's your responsibility to find something great in everyone you meet. It's not their responsibility to show you. Become curious. Stop being judgmental." ~ *Mark Manson*

I have a confession: I am a really good dancer. Both my brother

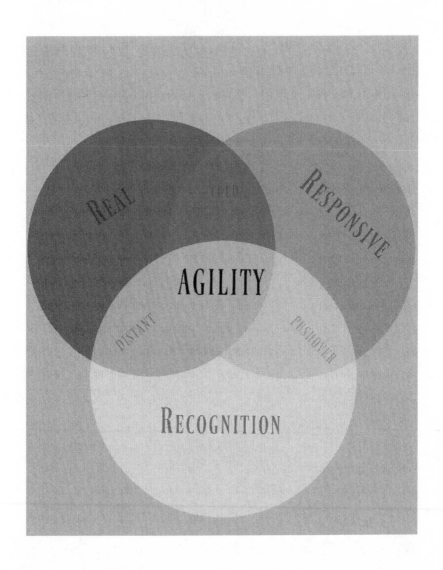

and girlfriend dance professionally, and it's hard to say who has influenced who more. I like to think they borrow a lot of my moves when crafting their own choreography.

On one cold October night in 2015 in St. George, Utah, I

finally got my opportunity. I linked up with a few of my girl-friend's co-workers and they taught me the moves I needed. I offered to add a little flavor of my own. Maybe the Wobble? The Electric Slide, perhaps? "No. Absolutely not." they said.

That's alright. Their loss. I was ready to perform on stage with a real live audience. It was my time to shine...

And shine I did. I killed it if I do say so myself (just don't ask anyone who was actually there...). Sure, a baby chimpanzee with only one leg could have performed the moves they taught me, but that's not the point. My 5 seconds of fame were something for the history books.

Can you tell how excited I was about my moment in the spotlight?

A few weeks after my performance, I was sharing this story with a friend of mine. As I'm sharing this with him, I notice him locked into his phone. He is delayed with "Uh-huh" and 'Yep" responses throughout my tale of glory.

So, I decide to stop talking. Halfway through the story I go dead silent.

He continues to scroll on his phone. I count out eleven seconds in my head. Eleven seconds feel like an eternity to sit in awkward silence.

He looks up at me, pauses for a second and goes, "Yeah man, totally..."

He had no idea that I stopped my story at halftime. How do you think that made me feel? I felt like I stepped into a pile of shit left behind by a Great Dane while wearing flip-flops.

In an age where we're continually swiping left, double tapping, and snapping photos, the first R of Social Agility is more valuable than ever. *Responsiveness* at its core is actively listening and appropriately reacting to others.

We all want to be valued and respected as individuals. Nobody wants to be treated like a number. Dale Carnegie—the OG Authority on social skills—says that one of his Three Fundamentals of Influencing is to make people feel important, and nothing makes people feel more valued, and valuable, than giving them your attention. We call it *paying* attention for a reason.

Attention has become such a limited resource that when we do give it to somebody else, they feel special. They feel noticed.

My man Harry T. Reis, a professor of psychology at the University of Rochester, ran a study called "Steps Toward the Ripening of Relationship Science." And when I say "my man" I mean I love him, and he has no idea who I am. Reis found that "If we want more connection, we have to be more responsive to others. Period... Our relationships are stronger when we perceive that our partners are responsive to us."

How do you know whether you're responsive or not? According to Reis, being responsive embodies three elements:

1. Understanding
"Seek first to understand, then to be understood."
~Stephen Covey, author, self-development OG.

Sam Walton, the founder of Walmart, was known to ask questions continually. He took trips to competitors' stores to study their tactics and strategies. He was even arrested in Brazil once for crawling around the floor with a tape measure. He was trying to figure out how far apart the aisles were spaced.

His management team would ask him why he didn't spend more time in his own store figuring out how to improve things? He would respond that he already knows everything that his stores do. He wants to learn new things that make his stores better.

And that's how I view empathy in Responsiveness: you already know everything about yourself. You know your story, your feelings, your interests—how you like your burger cooked, how many days in a row you prefer to wear the same underwear, why certain things make you upset— so spend time listening to and learning about others. Try to see the world through their eyes and understand how they feel.

What are their goals? Desires? Beliefs? What are they struggling through?

It's the ability to listen and understand, even when you come from opposite ends of the spectrum. It's the Democrat who genuinely tries to understand the Republican. It's being able to actively listen when they are explaining that floppy bacon is better, even when you *know* that crispy bacon is the only way to go.

Do you ask follow up questions? Do you actually hear what another is saying or are you planning out your next point? Do you paraphrase what they just said and repeat it back to them i.e., "It sounds like you're saying..."?

When we talk about ourselves and share our opinions, feelings, and ideas, it activates our brain's reward circuits the same way food and money do. So when you give somebody the stage and truly listen, they have all these feel-good chemicals flooding their brain. They then associate all those good feelings with talking to you. Even though you just sat there, they leave feeling positive vibes toward you.

But here's the caveat; you have to be genuine. People can sense disinterest. They can sense if you're using empathy as just another tactic. They know when you're just waiting for your turn to talk.

Empathy is not manipulative and it's not tactical. It's simply a way of being in the world. It is being interested, being curious, being in discovery mode.

In my coaching practice, my most successful calls involve giving very little actual advice. The most successful calls go like this:

Danny: What are you struggling with?

Client: I'm struggling with XYZ.

Danny: Tell me about that...

Client: **Talks for 10 minutes**

Danny: **Paraphrasing what they just said** "It sounds like you're saying XYZ."

Client: Yes! Totally. XYZ! Also, PDQ...

Danny: So, if I understand you correctly, you're struggling with XYZ and PDQ.

Client: YOU GET ME!

When we step outside our head and show others that we see their world and what's important to them, their perception of us transforms, and they feel as if we are truly connected, and so do we. As my father likes to remind me, "You have two ears and one mouth for a reason, my son. You should listen twice as much as you speak."

2. Validation

"Treat people as they are, no matter who they are, no matter where they sit in the world." ~ Jay Z

When you walk into a room, how do you feel? Do you feel like you're the man and the rest of us are scrubs? Do you think you're better than other people? Are you distinguishing between who's important and who's not? Do you treat people above you on the totem pole better than those below you?

These are mental filters of disrespect.

When we think and feel this way internally, others notice externally. People intuitively feel that you don't respect them. I was recently talking to a friend who said, "You know those name tag watchers at conferences?"

"What's a name tag watcher?" I asked, genuinely curious.

"You know, those people who walk by you and are trying to catch a peek at your name tag so they can see who you are and what you do," she said.

"Why do they do that?" I said.

"So they can decide whether or not to approach you."

Wow. I was shocked that people actually do this.

Research shows that the most reliable indicator of a healthy, romantic relationship is respect. When their partners talk, they listen. They see each other as smart, capable people. They validate their ideas and emotions with open, fair minds.

Want to know the formula for a failed marriage? Dr. John Gottman calls it the Four Horsemen of the Apocalypse. They are Criticism, Defensiveness, Stonewalling, and Contempt.

This is how we treat people we don't respect. We give them unwarranted feedback or don't give them the time of day.

The paradox about respect is that we often withhold it until we get it, but we cannot get it until we give it.

My most significant flaw is also my biggest strength: I'm a people pleaser. Not necessarily out of a need to be liked, or because I am afraid of conflict like a lot of my fellow people pleasurers, but because I genuinely *want* to be engaging with others. I enjoy spending time with people. I like hearing their stories. I genuinely love people. It makes me great at making friends, but my own productivity, daily agenda, and personal boundaries get taken over by others. This can lead me to feeling ashamed I didn't get any of my own work done or resentful of another person.

But more often than not, giving people the time of day has changed my life for the better.

The best piece of advice I ever received came from an older Greek man who, on the surface, had nothing to offer me. If I had a mental filter of disrespect, I would have walked right by him.

I was headed out of Starbucks with an afternoon coffee when somebody yelled out, "Hey! You. With the blue shirt." in the thickest Greek accent I ever heard.

"Yes?" I said.

"Do you play chess?"

"Not very well..."

"Ah, that's alright. Sit down and play," he said.

Before we began the game, he looked at me and said, "If I could tell you, young people, one thing, it's to do what you like. If you're not doing what you like, then you're wasting your time."

He then proceeded to beat me in about four moves and sent me on my way.

3. Caring
"We care more." ~ Seth Godin

My man Jade despises moving. Me? I've lived in a new house almost every year for the past decade. It's a way of life. Recently, I moved down the street from him.

I moved into a third-floor apartment in Los Angeles. I knew that my girlfriend and I wouldn't be able to move our

4-billion-pound mattress up three flights of stairs. Those Tempurpedics are worth the price for an amazing night of sleep, but are a total bitch to move.

Not sure what else to do, I called Jade and asked for his help. He didn't even blink. He came over right away.

We lugged that mattress up all 1,346 stairs. Jade was on the bottom pushing the bed up and, if you have ever moved before, you know that's the harder side. His face was bright red—we were both dripping sweat.

Jade's day was undoubtedly inconvenienced, and I can vouch that mattress was a pain in the ass. But he chose to help anyway, and I'll never forget it. Not only do I feel indebted to him, but it's cemented in my memory that he cares about me, that if I were in a time of need, he would be there to help.

The last aspect of Responsiveness is *caring*: taking active steps in helping and supporting others, meeting their needs, and giving in an unconditional way.

How often do you give with the expectation of having something in return? Do you feel like others owe you one? That isn't caring. That isn't forming genuine connections. That is transactional and manipulative.

I once (key word: *once*) had a friend who knew a ton about cars. I couldn't tell you the difference between oil and gas, but this friend could take a semi-truck apart and put it back together with a blindfold on. He offered to change the oil and air filters in my minivan (Yes, I drove a minivan in high school, and yes, the ladies loved it.) for free. It saved me money and the time of going to the dealership. I was extremely grateful.

Eight months later he needed a favor, so he humbly reminded me of that one time he worked on the van. Classy.

That's not caring; it's transactional. And it's how a lot of us operate in the world.

These are common neglect filters. When we don't care, it shows, and the other person takes notes that you are not someone that can be relied on.

We know that we truly care about someone when we give our own time, energy, and resources to help them achieve their goals, and expect nothing in return.

When you get to this point, people will feel it, and in return they will care about you. This leaves us feeling supported and satisfied with our friends and loved ones. It brings us closer together. When people care about us, we are better able to hear feedback and disagree because we know they have our best interest in mind. They have no intention of playing us or leaving us high and dry. This creates a connection that is unconditional, and there is nothing more powerful than that.

CONCLUSION

Responsiveness isn't a tactic; it's a religion. It's a way of being.

Authors Chip and Dan Heath write, "Responsiveness is not compatible with a canned agenda." There's no script. There are no pick-up lines. It's not a strategy to network with people who can do something for you. There's no formula. It's a way of being in the world.

It's having a certain genuineness about you. It's genuinely understanding, respecting, and caring about others.

How responsive are you? Do you remember the names of strangers you meet or forget instantly? Do you listen when others talk, or are you plotting on what you are going to say next? How much are you on your phone when somebody you know is talking? Do you ask follow up questions? Do you give without expectation? Do you show respect before you get it?

Once you begin being Responsive, you're in the game. But without the next elements of Social Agility, you'll be cast aside as a chump or a cold-hearted jerk.

Recognition

"You can make more friends in two months by becoming interested in other people than you can in two years by trying to get other people interested in you." ~ Dale Carnegie

There's this guy that used to work with my girlfriend at a dance company in Salt Lake City, and you can't help but want to be around the dude. He's the most magnetic, energetic person in the room. The dude glows, and everybody vies for his attention (including me). He makes you feel like you're "the one." He gives the most genuine compliments and shows love and interest in everyone he's around.

Last time I saw him, he was introducing me to people as a "brilliant writer."

I got B's & C's in English class my entire life. My girlfriend has to text me after every article I publish, showing my grammar and spelling mistakes. And this guy had me feeling like a cool blend of Ernest Hemingway and Mark Twain.

David Rock, the author of *Your Brain at Work*, writes about the needs of the human brain, and one of the biggest psychological needs of the human brain is "status." When we build people's status, they respond more favorably towards us. That's what this guy does to a T. He puts people in the spotlight. He makes them feel more significant than they see themselves.

It's hard to take ourselves out of the spotlight and put others in it because we feel like people won't see us, but that's not how it works. The more spotlights you set up on other people, the brighter yours gets.

My favorite writer, Mark Manson, often advises "One of my most common pieces of advice to men is that it's your responsibility to find something great in everyone you meet. It's not their responsibility to show you. Become curious. Stop being judgmental."

This skill, when developed, is one of the most powerful skills in creating genuine connection: being able to step out of our own heads long enough to notice and recognize another human being.

Author and Speaker, Zig Ziglar, says that most people walk into a room and say, "Here I am!" Great connectors don't do that. They walk into the room and say, "There YOU are!" This is the essence of Recognition; being able to switch from "look at me" to "look at you."

MY SAPPY CHRISTMAS CARDS

Every year, right after Thanksgiving, I take a weekend to myself. I bring my laptop and a list of names to a local coffee shop. That's it.

The names are of the people closest to me in life. They are family members, friends, and there are always a few new names of people who impacted my life over the course of that particular year.

I find a cozy spot in the corner, turn up the music on my headphones, open up a blank doc on my computer, and begin with the first name on the list...

I write them a letter. I delve into how I feel about them, things I've noticed about them that I appreciate. I show them love and gratitude and explain why I feel so lucky to have them in my life.

It's an emotionally heavy process. I always shed a tear or two, and I'm not the crying type. Well, at least not one that cries in a coffee shop type. For the next few weeks, I feel so full of love and joy.

It is some of my family members' favorite gifts. They think my actual gifts suck, but they look forward to my love letters.

I got the idea from Martin Seligman, one of the leaders of the Positive Psychology Movement. He calls these letters "gratitude visits." He suggests writing a letter of gratitude to someone, thanking him or her for what they do for you, or how they affect your life, and deliver the message in person.

His research found these letters are more impactful for those who write them than those who receive them. They can leave the author with a feeling of happiness for over a month.

Doug Conant, former President and CEO of Campbell Soup, wrote up to twenty handwritten notes per day to his employees.

These letters are Recognition at its finest. They show other people that you value them, which at the end of the day is all any of us really want. Complimenting people, and highlighting when they do something good, preferably at the moment, can have a profound impact.

Research shows that the #1 reason people don't like their jobs is lack of recognition.

We want people to perceive us as impressive, as different, or unique. The paradox is that the easiest way to be *interesting* is to become *interested* in others. Shine the light on them, and you'll reap the rewards.

The power of Recognition is twofold. First, when we shine

a light on others, we look more attractive through their lens. They develop positive feelings toward us, which makes them more open to supporting and loving us. This creates a feed forward cycle of mutual respect and support, two *huge* factors in developing relationships.

Second, it makes us feel better about ourselves. Giving others love and support moves our focus from ourselves to others. Jonathan Haidt, the author of *The Happiness Hypothesis*, says, "Giving help and support can be more beneficial than receiving it."

So on the quest to becoming Socially Agile, how often do you recognize others? Are you highlighting an employee's progress at work? Do you often tell your partner the things you love about them? Do you write thank you notes? Do you cry in coffee shops? An exercise I love is trying to give three compliments per day.

Bestselling authors, Chip and Dan Heath, say, "Recognition is universally expected, but not universally practiced." Be the leader in the field of recognition, and your relationships will thrive.

As my man Drizzy Drake says in his song, "Scholarships," "I need acknowledgment. If I got it then tell me I got it then."

You got it Drizzy... You got it...

Real

"We connect through sameness, but stand out through individuality." ~ Unknown, well maybe me? Probably not me.. Somebody said this... let's just say me.

There's a story that author and Navy SEAL, Mark Divine, tells about an experience he had in Officer Candidate School.

The Sergeant looked at Divine and barked out, "What do you stand for, Mark?"

"I stand for justice, integrity, and leadership," Divine replied.

"I didn't ask for your vanilla values, son!" The Sergeant screamed. "What are your rock-bottom beliefs that stand beyond which you won't be pushed? Don't just tell me what your family or society thinks you should believe in!"

I love this story because I think we all fall into this trap. We get so good at becoming attuned to the needs of others, that we neglect our own. We edit ourselves to suit everyone around us to the point that we begin to forget what we really think and believe.

The third part of Social Agility is the ability to be Real. If you are Responsive and Recognize others, you will undoubtedly be liked, but people will walk all over you. You'll be a pushover, unable to assert your true wants, needs, and identity, because you don't really know those things yourself. Like me, you'll end up talking in a coffee shop for six hours, and resenting others because you got none of your work done.

Who are *you*? What do *you* stand for?

Commonalities connect us, but authenticity is what makes us stand out. It's how we filter our Next Level Tribe. When we are our authentic selves, we attract the people that fit into our Tribe, and push away those who don't.

Even though there are 7 billion people in this world, you have a layer of individuality. It's truly amazing. However, most of us are conditioned to hide that element of originality, to fall in line. The problem with this sameness is that it's not particularly novel. You don't stand out.

Every year, a professor at the Wharton School of Business addresses students before they start the MBA program. He does an experiment where he asks what they want to do in their careers.

Most of the answers are about making a difference or doing something they love. Responses include things like being an entrepreneur, reforming healthcare, building websites, acting, or being a politician. Only a handful of people say investment banking or consulting.

Towards the end of the MBA program, the professor asks the same question.

This time, more than two-thirds of the group said they are planning to go into investment banking or consulting.

This is "herd mentality." The reason it's so dangerous is because it's subtle. Through dozens and dozens of nudges, we change and lose a sense of who we are, what we desire, and what we stand for. We adapt to fit in, not intentionally. It happens so slowly that we start to believe this is the "real us."

"Being Real" means acting authentically and having a set of personal values (And, not your vanilla values, son!).

Two-thirds of social skills are about letting others be the stars of the show. That's why the Social Agility model starts with Responsiveness and Recognition. But if we make everything we do 100% about others, then we're liable to get lost in the chorus.

IDENTIFY YOUR VALUES
In the 1990's, Stanford students kept journals over their winter break. Some were asked to write about any positive events that happened over the break. Others were asked to write about their values, and how their daily activities related to those values.

For example, Jade and I work out together a few times per week. So if I were in the positive events group, I would talk about how fun it was training with Jade, and how great I felt after the workout. But if I were in the values group, I'd write about how the workout was connected to my personal values of health and connection.

The students who wrote about their values showed better health and higher spirits when they returned to campus, and began to have a greater sense of meaning in their lives.

In the short term, these students felt more powerful and confident. They felt proud, secure, and more loving. They felt more connected to others, had more willpower, and even had an increased tolerance for pain.

Over the long term, writing about values was shown to increase GPAs, reduce doctor visits, and increase persistence. The craziest finding of all: People who wrote about their values only once for ten minutes had positive effects that lasted months, and in some cases, years later.

This is the first part of being Real: having a clear set of personal values. Values are not universal; they're individual.

Values act as our compass in navigating social relationships. They help us identify who is a good fit for our Next Level Tribe.

What words or ideas do you practice every day? What's your line in the sand? What do you stand for?

Jade and I call this The Honor Code – a list of powerful values that guide you in life. It's a statement of who you are in the world. We take every single one of our coaching clients through The Honor Code exercise.

Check it out –

BUILDING YOUR HONOR CODE

"The ultimate measure of a man is not where he stands in moments of comfort and convenience, but where he stands in moments of challenge and controversy. ~ Dr. Martin Luther King Jr.

If you're anything like me, you've skipped every exercise in every book you've ever read. True or true?

This is not one to skip. The Honor Code is your individual compass in life. It's what you go to when you have tough decisions to make. It's what you review when emotions are running high and you're not sure how to act. It keeps you doing the right thing, even when it's not what you *want* to do. It's your compass, made by you, for you.

Are you ready to do a book exercise for the first time in your entire life? Grab a pen and a piece of paper and go through the steps below.

1. Your Heroes

Who are the people you admire in life? Who would you love to meet? It doesn't matter if they are real or fake, dead or alive, or if you've met them or not. Write down the names of your heroes (aim to get at least three, but no more than 10). These could be people who are famous, historical or fictional (I won't lie, Professor Snape from the Wizarding World of Harry Potter made an appearance on my list ... don't judge). They can also be mentors, coaches, and other influential people.

For each hero, write 3–5 words that most embody their essence and the reason for your admiration. (So, if Professor Snape happened to make an appearance, you'd write "courageous" or "intelligent.")

What words would they use? Write these down.

2. Your Deathbed

You're lying down when your doctor comes in to let you know you only have a few hours to live.

How do you feel? Did you have a life well lived? What

made it so? What are some of your favorite memories? Do you have any regrets? What are they? What are the things you are most proud of? What are accomplishments that come to mind?

What words describe this? Write these words down.

3. Your Eulogy

Alright, I know this is getting depressing, but stay with me. Let's say those hours you had remaining from #2 above have expired. You have now died. I'm sorry. But I do have good news! You get the chance to sit in on your own funeral. Imagine you're a spirit sitting in the back of the room listening in on what people are saying about you. Maybe your mother or father are there, or your best friends from college. Maybe your children go up to say something, or the ladies from your local mahjong group. Wait, is that your personal trainer over there? Shit, she is going to tell everyone about your popcorn habit... And what? Your high school boyfriend who you haven't spoken to in years is here too?

You watch them all get up, one by one, and share some things about the person they knew. What do you want them to say? What sentiment would you be proud to have left? What words would they use? Write these down.

4. Your Anti-Values

You know how you just wrote about your heroes and all the traits that you admire about them? You did do that, right? Because we are actually doing this exercise, remember?

Now I want you to think about people you may not be so fond of. What are behaviors in those other people that you cannot stand? What are the words that come to mind?

Got them? Good, now write down the opposite of those words.

For example, here's what it might look like:

Quality You Dislike ⟶ Opposite
Arrogance ⟶ Humility
Animosity ⟶ Kindness
Jealous ⟶ Loving
Gassy ⟶ a Healthy Diet
Get it?

5. Now, take a look at the words, ideas, and descriptors you used in the thought experiments above. Do you notice any patterns or themes? Pull out five to ten of the words or ideas that repeat again and again.

6. From the isolated words, write a 3–10 sentence paragraph describing in detail who you want to be in the present as if it is you today. This is a description of your "superhero, Next Level self."

[As an example, we have included both my own, and Jade's honor code process— as well as an outline of this book's major insights and tools— in the Next Level Tribe Book Notes. You can access this for free by going to: www.nextlevelhuman.com/nextleveltribebook. Congratulations! You no longer have those vanilla values, son! Now you have a compass to work from.]

But even our Honor Code can be borrowed from people in our life. How do we know if this is genuinely what we stand for? How do we know that the herd mentality isn't creeping up on us?

Well, are you acting authentically?

LIVE AUTHENTICALLY

"I wish I dared to live a life true to myself, not the life others expected of me." ~ The most common regret of the dying (Bronnie Ware, Australian Hospice Nurse)

One of my best friends, we'll call him Jade, was 30 years old, and had recently graduated from medical school. He had just achieved his childhood dream of becoming a physician. He now had the distinct honor of wearing one of those little head mirrors and owing the government a quarter of a million dollars in student loans. That on top of credit card debt that made the Egyptian pyramids look modest.

Fresh out of school, a local health center in Seattle offered Jade a job to manage the facility. The starting salary would be $80,000/year. Not bad, right?

Except Jade was clear on who he was. He didn't go to med school to manage a health center. He declined the offer, moved home with his parents, and started his fitness business with nothing but a set of dumbbells and his mother as his first client.

The rest, as they say, is history. That decision led to a million-dollar company, a best-selling book, and a significant influence in the worlds of health and fitness.

I love this story because it shows clarity and perspective. The fact of the matter is that acting authentically is hard. As humans we are wired to care. We care about how our family and friends perceive us. We care about solving the stress and discomfort of the moment over our long-term futures. Like a ping-pong ball being smacked back and forth, we all will vacillate between being authentic and inauthentic. That's a normal part of living on this little blue marble. Sometimes we'll compromise our preference for the sake of someone else's. Sometimes we'll do something out of character. Sometimes we'll say something we do not mean, do something we shouldn't have done, or eat something we didn't even like. That's alright. That happens.

The problem is when we begin living truly inauthentic lives, and therefore lose ourselves (our individual interests, opinions, goals, values, and desires). We post the perfect picture on social media so strangers will think we're beautiful, and we slowly see the value of "being attractive" as important. We sacrifice our hopes and dreams to make somebody else happy, until we slowly boil in silent resentment. We constantly seek advice from others until we eventually value others' opinions of ourselves more than our own.

In the next section I will show you how to start acting more authentic in a way that attracts the right people into your Next Level Tribe.

Yes, it will be hard, but like Jade passing up $80,000 right out of medical school, those of us who can act authentically in the moment will attract the right people, and therefore, live a successful life in the long run.

So how can we know if we're acting authentically or not? Authenticity is when who you are on the inside matches up with what you say, and what you do, on the outside.

Let me break it down in a simple formula:

Authenticity = Clarity (of who you are) x Congruence (what you do and what you say).

CLARITY
You know that Honor Code we just built together? Really? You *still* didn't do it?! Would you please go back and do that freaking exercise? It's alright, I'll wait...

Did you do it? Wonderful.

Your Honor Code is a key piece of the Clarity puzzle. It's a reflection of your values and what you stand for. The reason we do exercises like this is because so many of us have no idea who our authentic self is. How can you act authentically when you don't know who you are?

Jade and I love the Osho quote, *"Your whole idea about yourself is borrowed-- borrowed from those who have no idea of who they are themselves."*

We borrow our values from our parents or our religion, and never question them. We borrow our interests and opinions from the friends we grew up with, without ever trying anything new. We set our goals based on others' expectations of us. This happens slowly and quietly until we wake up at 55 years old with a fire red Ferrari, a 21-year-old girlfriend who like, totally talks like this, a low back tattoo, and a whisky bottle that never leaves our side.

That is why authenticity is so hard, if we don't take the time to figure it out ourselves, we'll let others define us.

The Honor Code is just one piece of the Clarity puzzle. There are other things that we can do to become more absolute on who we are.

What are your interests? Here's a question that I always like to think about. How do you spend a Saturday afternoon to yourself? If you didn't have any responsibilities, how would you spend your time? Would you read? Write? Play sports? Meet up with friends? Taste wine? Pet chickens? How would you choose to engage with the world?

What are your goals? What are your opinions? What are your beliefs? And *why* do you believe what you believe?

These types of questions are just a starting point. The real clarity comes from actually engaging with the world. It comes from making decisions, following through, and then accepting whatever the consequences are. It comes from trying new things, exposing ourselves to new ideas, and stepping out of our daily comforts.

We can sit and reflect about who we are all day, but until we step outside, we'll never know for sure. The world is the greatest feedback tool we have. You may dream of being a doctor, but then the world "gives you" a bloody injury and you pass out. You may romanticize about retiring in Paris and spending your remaining days writing novels in small cafes off Rue des Martyrs, only to learn that being with your family is what makes you truly happy, and that writing is neither easy nor as pleasurable as you thought.

Engagement is the key to Clarity. Yes, ask yourself the questions, but then go out into the world and see if there is truth in your answers.

Like a beautiful Roman statue, your identity will slowly be chiseled and carved into a masterpiece that is uniquely your own and you'll learn exactly who you are.

And once you have Clarity, the challenging part of becoming authentic begins...

"[Too many people] have been caged into the same day-to-day grind, wasting away, spending their life doing things they don't truly enjoy, and that don't truly express their identity and personality." ~ Mark Manson

CONGRUENCE
"Being authentic is to believe everything you say and do."
~ Unknown

What if your authentic truth will shatter somebody else's world?

What if your values clash with the entire group around you? What if your interests create distance between lifelong friends?

These are the real-world challenges of acting authentically in a world that pushes back. Just because you read a book and wrote an Honor Code doesn't mean the world won't test that code.

This is the second, more challenging part of the Authenticity formula: *Congruence.*

Congruence is when you express yourself truly and fully, in both your words, and your actions.

Living congruently will cause a lot of short-term discomfort. There will be many growing pains and uncomfortable conversations. There will be judgment from those who do not align with your vision and changes in your external world.

But, like investing your money, Congruence will pay off in the long run. You begin to curate a circle of people who accelerate your growth and success: your Next Level Tribe. You'll start spending your days doing things you actually *want* to do, rather than a list of *have*-to-dos.

We all know when we are not living congruently. You know how you watch and make judgments about others based on what they say or do? Well, we do that to ourselves too. Our brain is watching and judging us just as we watch and judge others. It registers when we are not living in alignment with our values. It recognizes when we pursue a career that is not a good fit.

We are all going to slip up and not be Congruent at times. That's okay. The goal is not perfection, but improvement. That's why we write down our Honor Code and our goals, so we can review and practice them daily. Every single day the world will challenge you; that's the beautiful part of life. If you mess up, you'll get another shot at it tomorrow. The goal is to keep growing, to keep getting better.

The alternative is to continue living incongruently, hide our preferences, protect somebody else's feelings, or lower our boundaries for other people's comfort.

If we continue living inauthentic lives, we risk living with a lot of anxiety, depression, resentment, and regret, and then we die thinking, *"I wish I dared to live a life true to myself, not the life others expected of me."*

Conclusion: The Investment Relationships Take

In August 2015, a trip of a lifetime came to a close. My two brothers and I had traveled from New Jersey to Ireland to Paris to Brussels to Amsterdam to Berlin to Prague, back to Ireland and then, back to New Jersey.

It was nuts. We had so much fun, but the really interesting part was how well we all got along. We have an awesome relationship with one another, but when you put people together in close spaces for thirty straight days, add alcohol, navigation issues, and language barriers, even best friends may be ready to throw hands.

We had no issues. No arguments. No brawls. No irritability.

When my brothers and I were growing up, we would spend summers with our dad wherever he was that particular year.

No matter where he was living, we usually scheduled a few days to go to Maine, where his side of the family would congregate and rent cottages by the lake. It was a lot of fun.

One year, we were planning on skipping our Maine visit... until we weren't. We made the last-minute decision to make the run up to Maine in Dad's Dodge Durango to visit with the family. Unfortunately, because of the spur of the moment decision, there was little room for us to sleep.

My bros and I had to fold down the back seats of the

Durango and lay side-by-side with a single sleeping bag draped over the three of us. My dad reclined in the front seat.

If you know anything about Maine, you know that the state bird is the mosquito. So we had two options: 1) Keep the windows up and sweat profusely from the body heat and circulating breath from four humans piled into a Durango in the middle of July, or 2) Roll down the windows to cool off and get eaten alive by mosquitos.

Pick your poison.

My brothers and I had a lot of these "bonding" moments growing up. We'd have to entertain each other and make up games while we spent hours wandering around Wake Forest University waiting for my dad to get off work.

We slept in a construction trailer, the kitchen floor of a New York City apartment, and apartments with no furniture. That's A LOT of quality time.

Worse yet, my dad would make us give each other hugs when all we wanted to do was throw hands because "friends come and go, but family will always be there." Have you ever tried hugging somebody while your blood is boiling and all you want to do is hit them? It's anger management at its finest.

My mom had a strict "no hitting" rule. NEVER were we allowed to hurt each other physically. My dad had a "figure it out" rule because there was no freaking television or relaxing during summers when he was a kid in Dorchester, Massachusetts. Nah, you either went down to Waney Park to play basketball on the courts, covered with shards of glass, or you were down in Quincy Market selling papers for 8 cents apiece. "Oh, you're bored? Yeah, that's a luxury. "Figure it out," he would say.

So we did.

There are few people I could have been around for that

amount of time, in that limited space, and not have had at least some speed bumps. My relationships with my brothers are some of the strongest I have in my life.

But we *earned* it: because we went through the shit together. We've had the fights. We've seen the anger, the tears, the joy, and the pain.

Everyone wants solid relationships in life, but most of us aren't willing to put in the work that strong relationships require.

People want girlfriends/boyfriends but don't want to deal with the tears, uncomfortable conversations, insecurities and flaws of another.

People want true friendships, but don't want the inconvenience when a friend needs help moving or a ride to the airport.

Strong relationships take investment. Solid friendships take making sacrifices once in a while. Real connection can require hugging somebody when you want to punch them.

The problem with most social skills advice is that it comes with a list of tactics, but relationship building isn't a science; it's an art. It takes time.

It takes hundreds of moments of you being responsive to others. It takes a lot of recognition.

It takes stripping away your barriers and being your authentic self, being real. It requires figuring out what you stand for and who aligns with you.

It takes being Socially Agile. It takes effort and time.

Then one day, you'll find yourself in Prague with a plate of fish that still has its head and eyes intact, and a round of large beers for $4.80, and laughing about that one time you all slept in that Dodge Durango.

PART 3

• • •

Finding Your Tribe

By Jade Teta

"Think for a long time whether or not you should admit a given person to your friendship. But when you have decided to do so, welcome them heart and soul, and speak as unreservedly with them as you would with yourself."
—Seneca—

The Social Battery: Amplifying Your Social Charge

• • •

had just moved to Los Angeles from North Carolina. I spent my first week there at the local Equinox, an exclusive, high-end gym. It was just like all the other gyms I spent most of my life in, except more polished with more "upscale" clientele. I used to love these types of gyms, a big open floor with a ton of equipment; everyone focused and engaged with their workouts. People were zeroed in on what they were there to accomplish; heads down, music blaring in their ear buds.

Those headphones might as well have been blinders too, because no one was interacting. It was a strange thing for me to notice. In the past, I was the guy with my head down and the music cranked up. Now I was looking to connect. I was trying to get a sense of the people and the energy in my new town. Needless-to-say, I was not loving this gym. I thought to myself,

"We are all together, in this big room of equipment and yet, there is no sense of belonging."

At the same time, I was thinking, "Man, who are you? You used to love this aspect of the gym." To me, back then, gyms were a place to work out, not talk. In fact, I would be annoyed if my workout got interrupted by a conversation. I was seeing things differently now. I still did not want my workout interrupted, but I was craving some kind of connection. For the first time in my life, I felt like I did not belong in the gym. I was not ready to give up on all gyms, but I had enough of that one.

On my walk back home, I passed another gym. It was a CrossFit Center. I had done some CrossFit workouts before, but had never been to one of the gyms (boxes in CrossFit lingo). If you have never heard of CrossFit, it is a gym built around community. Everyone does the same workout together. I had avoided places like CrossFit because it did not really speak to my strengths. I was a powerlifter and bodybuilder; at CrossFit you lift weights, but you do a lot of other things too.

The next day I was at my first workout. The workout included fifteen other people. We all shook hands and chatted before the start of class. Then the workout started. It was crazy intense, my kind of workout. You could not talk to the person next to you even if you wanted to. But as some people started to finish their workouts, they began to cheer on the people still finishing theirs. Since I was unaccustomed to this workout, I was definitely taking up the rear.

A word of advice: Never do someone else's workout if you don't want to have the shit beat out of you. I was not accustomed to either this style of training, nor this kind of athletic team atmosphere in a gym.

After the workout people sat around and chatted. There

were actors, musicians, financial types, programmers, and others. These were well-off, well-educated, seriously creative types, who loved their work and lived the fit lifestyle. My younger self probably would have hated all this, but the side of me that was craving a Tribe of creative professionals felt like he was immediately at home.

This is the first rule of finding a Next Level Tribe. Go to the places that contain the type of Next Level Humans you would like to be. I had just found one of those places. I left that CrossFit workout centered and charged up. In the past, I may have been able to recharge myself, but in my new, unstable state, I needed a little social jumpstart. I had just discovered one place to get it.

You may not think of it this way, but your social, emotional and spiritual self is like a battery. It can be charged up, and it can be drained.

Your Tribal Charge

Imagine you are walking around outside with your cell phone; the battery is low, and just as you are typing out a text reply, it goes black and dies. Now imagine that instead of charging it up, you walk up to your family and friends, angrily shove the phone in their faces and say, "Why did you not make sure my battery was charged? You never charge my phone! Why am I always left with a phone at close to empty with zero charge?"

Or maybe you just stare helplessly at the darkened screen and lament how you have no charge. Thinking no one is ever there to charge your phone for you.

Or perhaps you just ignore the fact your phone died and simply put it in your pocket. Dejected, you decide you don't need the phone at all. The phone always lets you down anyway.

You resolve that you will get by without the phone. You decide the phone is not worth it. No one will charge it anyway, and it always creates problems for you. You resign yourself not to ever use the phone again.

I realize each of these scenarios sounds ridiculous—when most people notice they have low battery they just find the nearest outlet and plug in—but as insane as those reactions seem, they are not too far from how many people behave when it comes to their social interactions.

It is not another person's responsibility to make sure your social, emotional and spiritual batteries are charged. At the same time, you can't ever hope to charge up fully without the involvement of others at times. That's the dilemma.

Other people can act as a significant source of your social charge, but also may drain your social batteries.

You must understand this dual nature of people, and their impact on your energy reserves. You are the one responsible for the people in your life. You teach them how to treat you. You must start to view the people you spend time with as either net positive or net negative influences. You need to flesh out when and where to include them in your life.

Some people will provide insight regarding finances. Some individuals will inspire you to get healthier and fit. One friend will be someone you can lean on emotionally, someone else might stir your intellectual juices, and another friend might be the perfect person to laugh, let loose and have a few beers with. Some people will charge you up and others will drain the shit out of you. You need to know which are which.

Have you ever even thought about that?

Like it or not, you are a social being above all else. You can no longer be in the dark about the other people in your life and their impact on you. You can't leave your social, emotional and spiritual charge to chance.

If you hope to elevate your life and get to your Next Level, you must take full control over your social battery and Tribe.

The Social Tribe

Imagine you are a member of an ancient hunter-gatherer tribe. There are just shy of thirty people in your group, including you. All of these people are like family to you, except not all of you are related. This Tribe is all you know. It is who you are. You have your own personality, and your Tribe knows you as that individual person. But your Tribal identity is just as important, in fact more so.

The Tribe comes first. Putting your needs above the tribe makes no sense, because your survival depends on your group. You have little choice but to put your personal needs aside. Not doing so could spell disaster for you and everyone else.

You must work together with your tribe because you inhabit an uncertain world where humans are not at the top of the food chain. A human going at it alone is a dead human.

This is why we are such social creatures. It is built into our physiology like computer software.

You inherited the need to be a part of a group; this is why you care so deeply about what other people think of you. This is why it hurts so badly to not be included, to be talked about behind your back, to lose a friend, or to go through a breakup. Everything about you seeks to be a part of a group.

Groups exert powerful influence over us. They influence our thoughts, beliefs, behaviors and values. Most people find a group, and try to become a member. The better way to do this is to decide the Next Level Person you want to become, and create a Tribe that helps you elevate to that level.

This is what is meant by "Next Level Tribe." It is a group you have created and cultivated that supports you in your growth as a human. You support your Tribe members as well. A Next Level Tribe is a synergistic unit that grows as a whole due to the elevation of the individuals in the group.

This type of group collaboration, where the individual's growth is given priority over the collective, is different than most groups. Just as there are Base Level and Culture Level human tendencies, there are also Base and Culture Level groups.

A Base Level Group is about survival and the Group comes first. In fact, individuals are seen as subordinate to the Group and are punished for having individual goals and concerns. These groups are formed by people who feel threatened in some way and seek like-minded, easily influenced individuals who can be controlled, and who are also willing to fight with them. Fight who? Any group or individual who is different in any way. Being different is dangerous to a Base Level Group.

Examples of these Groups exist throughout history. Modern day extreme versions can be found in terrorist groups, cults, the alt-right racists and alt-left anarchist movements. More subdued examples include shit-talking groups of teenagers, bullies, and family or work environments where shit-talking and back-stabbing coalitions are the norm. A Base Level Group is usually formed to resist change and/or force individuals to conform to the beliefs of the Tribe. If you are not part of the Tribe, you are an enemy. These Tribes have a rigid set of rules, an unfaltering view of the world and a "you are either with us or against us" mentality. A Culture Level Tribe is more about fitting in. It is also about status or finding a place to feel safe, in the know, and justified. Culture Level Groups are extremely common, and are most easily seen in the realms of politics and religion. These Tribes are all about championing what they believe, and reinforcing that their way is the best, most rational way. They want to exclude. The "fake news folks" on the right and the "politically correct police" on the left are examples. When a person's own values of honesty, balance, and truth are put aside in the name of the Tribe, they have been hijacked by Culture Level "group think." These Tribes have a "we are better, smarter, and more virtuous than they are" mentality.

Modern day examples of Culture Level Tribes can be seen in political coalitions. It is common for members of political parties to attack those of the opposite party as misguided, ignorant, immoral, and confused. However, when leaders of their own party exhibit the exact same behaviors, they suddenly fall silent and make excuses. When a family-values Christian attacks Barack Obama for his supposed immorality, yet says nothing about Donald Trump's questionable behavior, you are seeing Culture Level Tribe dynamics play out. When a progressive Democrat attacks George Bush for his supposed involvement in 9/11, and Hilary Clinton is assumed a saint, with little consideration given to her potential shortcomings, Culture Level Tribe behaviors are evident.

A Next-Level Tribe is completely different. It has its members' personal growth as the ultimate goal. Its charter is not to fight other groups, or prove they are smarter than others, but rather to work on expanding the group's collective intelligence. They do this by recruiting Next Level Individuals, who bring insights and expertise that make the group better. This generates a compound learning effect where all Tribe members benefit by accelerating their personal growth beyond what an individual could achieve alone. This type of Tribe is committed to growth and learning. Each member of the group is encouraged to seek their highest level as individual humans. The belief is that "when you grow, I grow and when we grow, they grow."

The Next Level Tribe has the mentality that we are all in this together. A Next Level Tribe member strives to be the best person they can be so that they are in a position to help their Tribe members excel as well. It is the Tribal equivalent of the airplane oxygen mask; put your mask on first so you can assist the members of your tribe when they are struggling.

The key distinguishing factor of a Next Level Human, and the Next Level Tribes they form, is that life is about learning, teaching, and sharing. We do not, and cannot, know everything, but when we as individuals seek to grow, and allow others to grow as well, our learning as a culture is amplified and everyone benefits as a result. In this way, a Next Level Group seeks members who expand the group awareness to build a community that evolves past tribal dynamics. Next Level groups don't have an "us versus them" mentality, but rather a "we are on the same team" viewpoint. Bias and dogma are seen as contrary to everything the group stands for. Open mindedness, tolerance, growth and common humanity are seen as the ultimate virtues in a Next Level Group.

Another way to conceptualize the ideal dynamics of a Next Level Tribe is the modern-day sports team. Whether it is American football, basketball, baseball, soccer or hockey, individual players are expected to perfect their position and play that position to the best of their ability. When one player does their job, it makes the other team members' jobs easier. This then creates a positive environment whereby the entire team benefits and excels. When individual players are free to exhibit their best performance, it elevates the group's play. It is a virtuous growth cycle.

In team sports, there is no selfishness; people play for themselves and the team simultaneously. There is also no dishonesty. Players tell each other the truth. They simultaneously demand you take responsibility for yourself while being willing to pick up the slack if the team requires it.

Sure, there are superstars on any team, but those stars shine only when they embrace the Tribe and the Tribe embraces them back. That is how you want to think about creating your own Next Level Tribe.

So, what is your favorite team sport? American football? Major League Baseball? Rugby? Basketball?

Imagine you get hired as the head coach and general manager of a professional sports team. Your job is to create the best team possible for success.

You must first assess the players on your current team to determine if they are helping or hurting the team's efforts. Do you need to move players around to positions better suited to them? Do you need to recruit new players?

This is exactly what you must do with your Social Tribe. You have to take a good, hard look at how your current Tribe is constructed. Is it charging your battery or draining it? Is it a winning team that can take you to the championship, or a Tribe of emotional scrubs that will keep you at base level?

The first step is understanding which positions are most important for your social, emotional, and spiritual well-being.

I want to help you do that with an exercise I call the Tribal MVPs. These are the most valuable players on your Tribe's team

There are five major types of people you need in your Tribe: Supporters, Believers, Counselors, Coaches & Mentors

SUPPORTERS

As humans, we need to feel safe and supported. Does someone have your back? Do you feel like you belong somewhere? Do you feel like you matter to anyone? If you were in financial trouble and needed a place to stay, is there someone that you could go to?

The people who are your ride or die peeps, the ones you would not hesitate to call, those are your Tribe. It is not just about that they "get you," it is more about that they "got you." It doesn't matter if time has gone by, you had words in the past, or others are attempting to stand in the way, these people will show up if you ask and will ask for nothing in return. Supporters are critical, and this group of people is usually the closest members of your Tribe. We need these people in our world and they are the physical embodiment of support.

Other people are in your world as well. You are in their sphere of awareness and they are in yours. You may run into them at the grocery store, engage with them at your kid's little league game, bump into them at the coffee shop, or see their likes and comments on your social media posts. They may be pleasant but their attention, promises, and words of affirmation are empty. They offer no real support.

These are the opposite of supporters, and the last ones you want in your Tribe. We call these people the Empty Audience. They are watching, but they've got nothing for you. They can be a pleasant distraction, and maybe nostalgic or fun to be around but in the end, they provide only empty platitudes.

These types are more prevalent today because social media has expanded our sphere of awareness. Very few of the hundreds of social media friends and followers are Tribe members. Most of them are the Empty Audience.

It's important to keep the Empty Audience out of your Tribe. Just because someone is in your social sphere of awareness does not mean they are Tribe members. In fact, they can be the very thing keeping you from creating a Next Level Tribe.

As humans, we care deeply about what other people think and how they feel about us. Many of us develop the bad habit of trying to please people who we barely know, or even like. When we focus our attention on the Empty Audience, we can easily turn our attention away from the people whose time and attention matter most to us.

BELIEVERS

We all have dreams and aspirations. That is part of what it means to be human. They may be silly daydreams, like sipping a Mai Thai on the beach with our beautiful Latin lover. They could be big dreams like speaking on stage to thousands who are lifted and inspired by our message.

What may be more important is believing in other people's dreams. I call this the Morpheus Principle after the fictional character from *The Matrix* movie trilogy. The name, "Morpheus," refers to the Greek god of dreams and sleep from Ovid's *Metamorphoses*.

In the films, Neo is the chosen one; only he does not know it. Morpheus sees it in him. Not jealous or envious, Morpheus knows his role. He wants nothing more than for Neo to realize his power. Morpheus' belief in Neo is so strong that he sacrifices his own life so that Neo can discover the truth of his power.

The name Morpheus is telling. He can "morph" people into believers in themselves. As humans, the most important thing we can have is belief in ourselves. Psychology research has discovered the three most essential elements for success in life: 1) belief in ourselves 2) the belief others have in us, and 3) our ability to see stress, hurt, and suffering as growth promoters.

All three of these have an element of other within them. If we see people who strongly believe in themselves, it can inspire us to believe in ourselves as well. Having a strong support system makes us feel more confident in our abilities, and more likely to take the risks necessary to succeed. If we see someone else confront their fears, fall and get back up, we can learn through their experience that failure does not have to kill you, but instead can make you stronger.

Belief in self is easier when you have members of your Tribe who exhibit belief in themselves, thereby providing examples and models to consider. From them you can see what authentic confidence looks like, be more likely to emulate, and eventually integrate, this critical personality trait. This is also true of using stress, trials, and tribulations as personal growth accelerators. You see how they think and act when they are going through hard times. This then becomes your way of behaving too. Of course, when other people believe you can do it, you are far more likely to believe in yourself and others too.

Growing up, I had confident older brothers and an older sister showing me the way as I followed in their footsteps. Their confidence helped me believe in myself. They also modeled resilience and provided me with examples of how to grow from failures, and confront my fears.

I have been fortunate to have a family who has always believed in me, even when I did not believe in myself. The gift they gave me in that regard was so strong that I have become the Morpheus figure for so many others as a result. Showing others how to believe in themselves and their potential has been something I now embrace fully. It has even become the driving force in my career pursuits.

I call these types your Believers. That is the part they play in your Tribe.

Who are the people in your world who see your power and believe in you even more than you believe in yourself? Who are the people who know you can do it, even when you are in doubt? Who are those who believe so strongly in themselves that you are inspired to believe in yourself too? These are your Believers, and you need them in your Tribe.

Not everyone is a Believer. In fact, many people will feel threatened by your dreams. They haven't achieved their dreams, so they don't believe you can achieve yours. They gave up on their dreams, and so perhaps hope you too will fail.

These types are some of the hardest people to deal with, and oftentimes the people we are closest to. Some of our close family members and friends, more often than we would like, play this role.

It is frustrating, I know, but we must remember that people crave certainty and comfort above all else. You trying to be something more significant and grow yourself is an unsettling force in their certain world. This is why they are threatened by your daring to achieve or be something more. Whether they love you or not, these are the Haters.

Haters will tell you it can't be done. They will tell you it is not realistic. They will tell you not to aspire beyond your station. When you hear things like this, it's tempting to think that they really are talking about you. After all, they are directing their comments toward you, and they even believe they are talking about you. But you should know better.

Understand that when Haters make these statements, they

are really expressing their own fears, obstacles, and internalized messaging. What they are conveying is they are too afraid, and you should be too. Think about it. If you succeed, what does that make them think of themselves?

You can feel sorry for a Hater. You can listen to a Hater. You can even try to understand a Hater. But never internalize what they are saying. That stuff is more about them than it is about you. By believing in yourself and authentically owning who you are and what you are about, you inspire others to begin to see themselves as capable as well. By supporting others, and seeing their power and strengths, you help them develop that same skill and become a Morpheus figure themselves.

Remember your Tribe. Stick close to your Tribe's MVP's and avoid emotional scrubs like Haters. How can you hope to make it to the championship if no one on in your Tribe believes it is possible? You need to cut the Haters and draft the Believers.

COUNSELORS

Emotions are tricky. Some are like the weather, unpredictable and dangerous. Other emotions are a peaceful, steady path leading to where you are headed and what you must learn. Stuck emotions, the type that recur over and over, are a warning sign that you are at a dead end, and may need to turn around. The goal with emotions is to use them as information. Once you have declared where you want to go, emotions can help you understand your current location. Thought of the correct way, emotions are like the Google Maps of your psyche.

You might think you want members of your Tribe who make you feel warm and fuzzy all the time. What you want are those who make space and time for your emotions and who can weather your emotional storms to help you see where the feelings are pointing you. Sometimes this means they challenge you and push you. It may not feel good in the moment, but in the long run, this helps you grow and get better as a human.

There was a time when I was having a difficult issue with an ex-girlfriend, who I wanted to remain friends with. I was hurt at how she was treating me. I had done my best to support her in her new relationship and be a good friend. But everything I did seemed to backfire. Instead of being grateful and thanking me, my efforts made her more distant and hostile. I went into a long diatribe about all the things that were going wrong. I felt taken advantage of. I was hurt by something that was said. I had a bunch of other concerns. At times I felt like she was blaming me for difficult things that were happening in her life.

One of my closest bros sat me down and listened. He did not try to solve my problem. He recognized my venting was a necessary clearing and recalibrating. He recognized my behavior as healthy and justified. He made the space, and gave me his most valuable asset: time.

He said little. He reinforced that he understood and could see why things were tough. He asked clarifying questions and I repeated what I was expressing. The questioning and paraphrasing showed he was listening.

He also gave me the number one thing a person is looking for when they vent: empathy. He said, "Wow, I can see how that would feel so shitty. I get it. I am not sure I could have handled it as well." These were not empty platitudes—he truly felt this way.

Fifteen minutes went by. I had come full circle and developed clarity. He was my sounding board and reflection point. I felt better and altered my psychological compass as a result.

There have been other times with this same friend when he pushed me a little more. He did not agree with my point of view or felt I was being too narrow-minded in my perspective. Those discussions were a little testier and stressful for us both, but the outcome was the same: more clarity and understanding.

Because his intention was not to be right, but rather, to help; he was able to reveal my blind spot. This did not mean I agreed with his point of view, but his perspective did help me recognize some of my emotional blocks, and moved me closer to resolution and growth.

I was not able to find clarity in the initial emotional trigger. As my close friend, he was able to see my blind spot, the same way I often notice his. That is what makes intimate relationships our best teachers.

We cannot see our own blind spots, but those closest to us can. As long as they are Next Level Humans, who are interested in growing us, there is no greater social asset.

These are the types of friends we need in our lives. They let us vent, but they don't allow us to become victims. I call these people Counselors. Sure, this could be an actual, trained counselor you hire, but your friends can act this way too. You can be a Counselor to them as well.

These types make us feel better and clearer. We usually leave the conversation feeling lighter, fresher, and enhanced as people. They provide us with more clarity of where we need to go and grow.

These types don't always say what we want them to, and they may not always agree with our point of view, but they are still there for us. They are not there to be right and prove us wrong, but instead, help us see what we are not able to understand on our own.

The opposite of Counselors are Vampires. They suck the emotional life out of us. They overpower us with their own emotions—never allowing us time or space to get a thought or feeling in—or they find a way to turn our emotions back to them. These types always seem to be carrying emotional baggage. They not only want to tell us all about their baggage, but they want us to carry it for them.

If you want to know if someone is a Counselor or a Vampire, look at whether they carry baggage or set up boundaries.

"Boundaries over baggage" is a great mantra to remember. Counselors have firm boundaries, and they expect you to have them as well. They don't let you step over their boundaries, and they are careful not to infringe on yours. What do I mean by boundaries? They are those personal lines in the proverbial sand. The lines that you don't allow others to cross, that define how you expect others to treat you in terms of kindness, honesty, respect and other core values.

My ex-wife and close friend, Jill, and I talk about this a lot. We often hear couples say some of the rudest and most demeaning things to each other. We never did that when we were married, and we don't do it now. Both of us have very strong boundaries around how we allow others to talk to and treat us. If you say something disrespectful to Jill or me, it may be the last time you say anything to us at all; as we are likely to eliminate you from our Tribe. It is a boundary we simply do not allow others to cross. We treat others with respect, and expect them to do the same.

Counselors don't allow you to wallow in "victim." They call you back to yourself with honest compassion and force you to get in touch with your boundaries.

Vampires drop their baggage on top of your boundaries. They will try to suffocate you with their emotional baggage if you let them. They complain, blame, manipulate, and, at their worst, wound and attack. Not unlike their namesakes, they feed off of your life force—off of your emotional resources. They leave you feeling drained and empty.

To deal with a Vampire, all you need to do is become a Counselor. Create boundaries that do not tolerate any encroachment. They will either have to honor your boundaries or be unable to interact with you. It is a perfect vetting system, and the only way you can rebuild and protect your emotional reserves.

COACHES

My family is amazing. They are my social, emotional, and spiritual rocks. Even when I have not talked to them in months, I am bolstered by knowing they are there. My mother especially plays this role. But they also have a downside for me.

My family loves to eat. We are a big Italian family who prefers to sit around eating, drinking and talking. Some families will go on a hike together or work out together. Not mine. We eat.

They know I like cake and cookies, so they give me cake and cookies. And believe me, I want the cake and cookies. At the moment, I love the sugar rush and stuffing my face like a little kid, but when I get home after a weekend of hanging with them, I am bloated, tired, unmotivated, and useless.

In this state, I am convinced the only suitable thing for me to do is give up and be a professional parade blimp. It can take weeks to get back to feeling healthy after hanging with my family.

Our physical health and fitness relate directly to our mental and emotional stamina and resilience.

Health and fitness researchers have determined that being overweight and unhealthy is contagious. We tend to be about as fat and sick as the five to ten people we spend the most time with.

Our championship Tribe needs people who help us eat better, work out regularly, and take care of our physical health. I call these types Coaches. They could be a hired coach, like a personal trainer or nutritionist, but it's better to have your closest friends acting as Coaches.

Instead of sitting down to dinner, ordering bacon-wrapped potatoes smothered, slathered, battered and deep-fried, we need people who help us order salads. We need people who invite us to hike and bike, not drink and eat.

Those who move us toward our health and fitness goals are Coaches, and the people who move us away from those goals are Enablers. Enablers are often well-meaning, but misguided. The good news is, Enablers often want to be helpful and can frequently be turned into Coaches by simply communicating what you need. You need plenty of Coaches in your social circle if you plan on being vital, healthy, and fit, now and throughout life.

MENTORS

You ever heard anyone say, "Man those were the good old days?" Have you ever thought that yourself?

There is a reason people look back at certain times in their lives with that kind of nostalgia. It's because that was a time when they were engaged in life.

Think about the ages from 15 to 30 years old. You are finding yourself. You're going to school and learning. Playing sports or learning an instrument. Some friends come and go. You fall in love. You fall out of love. You go to college. You learn a trade. Perhaps you get married. Maybe you have kids. There are new jobs. Maybe travel, if you can afford it. Managing life, managing people and all the rest.

Then, all that action starts to happen less and less. Things get routine. Things get stale. Monotony sets in. Before you know it, the passion is gone and seems difficult or impossible to recapture.

Next thing you know, you are longing for something else. You don't know what that "something else" is, but you want it nonetheless.

But why? Why do we feel like we are no longer alive, or lost? What causes this?

Being human is what happened. We have built-in desires for both stability and variety.

Humans have a natural tendency to seek comfort and security. That makes sense. That is what all the learning and hard work was for, right? We work hard, we struggle, we suffer, and as a result, we should earn our comfort and stability.

But then we come to a frightening realization; too much comfort and stability sucks. So, in response to that, we seek excitement, pleasure, and entertainment. We seek out social media, reality TV, computer games, stirring up drama, affairs, adult toys, like boats, sports cars, and all the rest.

Of course, none of this quite does it. We still feel empty.

I have a quote framed and hanging in the center of my living room. It is the first thing I see when I walk down my steps in the morning. It's by the poet Rumi and it says, "The Lion Is Most Handsome When Hunting For Food."

I get asked about its meaning by many of my guests. Being in pursuit of something is when we are most alive, most beautiful and most in our power. What Rumi is saying is, that the longing and the chase are what make something attractive to us. It is what makes us beautiful to others as well. This is the principle of engagement.

Martin Seligman, the father of happiness psychology, says that engagement is a crucial determinant of success and happiness. The least engaged individuals are the least happy individuals.

I conceptualize engagement in a very simple two-word mantra: "change and challenge." We often feel stale and lost because we become afraid of change and avoid challenge.

We admire others who make changes in their lives and take on challenges; praising a friend who leaves an oppressive marriage to be single in their 40's, and envying a coworker who quits their desk job in a magnificent blaze of glory to open a yoga studio. All the stories we love involve change and challenge, and yet, when it comes to our own lives, there is a barrier of fear and discomfort that keeps us stagnant.

Intuitively, we know that change and challenge are what grow us, make us love life and keep us hungry to pursue what's next. Yes, change and challenge are hard, but it's even harder when we go at it alone. This is why our social circle needs those who expose us to new places and new things. This is why we need friends who force us out of our comfort zones.

I call these types Mentors. A Mentor can be someone we hire, like a life coach. We can also find mentors by joining a Mastermind (a group of supportive, like-minded individuals pursuing similar goals), but having friends who act as mentors is one of the most abundant sources of growth.

Mentors expose us to things we didn't know we didn't know. They provide opportunities for exploring new places, new things, and new ideas.

My father came from a very conservative and stable family, while my mother came from a liberal and unstable one. The two of them have a fantastic relationship and have remained married for 50 years. My father is 75 and my mom is 71.

I remember when I was a teen, my mother would come home and triumphantly announce to my dad, "Jimmy, don't make plans for Thursday. You have a pottery class."

One week it would be pottery. The next week it would be stone cutting. The following month it would be meditation and a yoga retreat.

My father would complain and get pissed off. I still laugh to myself when I imagine his voice saying, "Jesus, Joyce! Stop signing me up for shit all the time."

But he would always go, be challenged and learn. He resisted at first, but in the end, he was enhanced. My mom forced him out of his comfort zone. If you ask him about it today, he says, "We always did a lot of fun things both together and apart. We kept exposing each other to new things."

Today my father is still being pulled out of his comfort zone by my mom and by us, his kids. But he has now begun to take on the Mentor mantle and pulls us out of our routines. He recently planned a two-week trip for the family to hike 170 miles through Portugal and Spain!

Mentors grow you and show you. They expose you to all the things your spirit wants and needs but did not know existed. You must have these people in your life.

Victims are the opposite of Mentors. They want you to stay still. They want to trap you in an illusion of comfort and stability. For a victim the world is dangerous. You could get hurt.

Planes crash, so let's not travel. Learning the piano costs money, so let's not do it. A self-development seminar is silly, that is what religion is for. Talk? Communicate? Why?

Victims are those who don't want to feel fear and will do everything they can to avoid failure. They want to sit on the sidelines and play it safe.

Mentors are those who help you conquer fear by confronting it. They help you understand that failure is the greatest learning opportunity we humans have.

The motto of a Victim is, "Better safe than sorry."

The motto of a Mentor is, "Play it too safe and you will be sorry."

Life is nothing if not change. To stay the same is to stop living. Mentors help you elevate your experience.

You know you need a Mentor in your life when following a sports team or watching a show on Netflix is more exciting to you than your own life.

Recruiting Your Next-Level Tribe

Now that you understand the different positions your Tribe needs, I want to discuss how you're being drained or charged.

This is where you are going to do some work. Take a look at the battery diagram below. We have filled in all five positions. We separated the categories so you can see the positive and negative sides of the battery.

The Tribal Battery

PEOPLE	**+**	**—**
	TRIBE	EMPTY AUDIENCE
	BELIEVERS	HATERS
	COUNSELORS	VAMPIRES
	COACHES	ENABLERS
	MENTORS	VICTIMS

Your Social Tribal Charge

We humans spent most of our evolution in small bands of hunter-gatherers between 20 and 50 people. This is still a pretty good guide as to how many people we have in our social sphere today.

We may have hundreds, or even thousands, of people as social media "friends," but only a small amount of people occupy any mental/emotional capital.

Modern-day makes this a little tricky because we can be socially engaged without having many people around us physically. Social media makes it so we are seeing, and being seen, while not actually being in front of people. We can debate this modern-day predicament, but you are investing social capital into these relationships whether you spend physical time with these people or not.

We can also be attached to someone who may not even know us at all, think authors we read, influencers we follow, and celebrities we study. Again, these people may not know or be aware of us, but they occupy a place in our social energy system nonetheless.

Assessing your current Tribal Charge

With these considerations in mind, and referring to the Tribal Battery diagram above, I want you to write down the top twenty people who occupy your social, emotional and spiritual space. Remember, these should be actual people in your life. Leave your chosen god outside of this exercise.

Also, fictional characters are not involved either. You might feel like you and Jon Snow from *Game of Thrones* are BFFs, but trust me he is too busy fighting White Walkers to care much about what you are doing.

Historical figures don't make the list either, even those whose work influences you. For example, I spend a reasonable amount of time reading authors from the past. Some of them act as mentors to me in a way. However, they are not real people I know who influence me in any way. I would not want to include them.

This exercise itself can clue you into some things. If you end up wanting to add 20 historical figures in your social circle and no real people, you need to get out more. The true essence of a Next Level Tribe is having actual, flesh and blood members.

Let me give you a sense of how this might work for me. I am very close to my immediate family. There are five of them. All of them are alive (my parents, two older brothers and an older sister). They are with me always. The energy of them is there despite not being physically in my same city.

So they would make up five of my twenty. My close friends make the list. Danny is one of my closest friends, so he is in my twenty. My other very close friends make up about another five people.

Now things get a little trickier. I still often check in on (read: *spy on*) my ex-lover on social media and try to see what she is up to. She makes the list even though we don't talk at all because of the time I spend thinking about her and checking up on her.

For a time I was checking up on her boyfriend on social media too. I don't know him personally, and we have never met. Yet, there was a time where he occupied some of my social, emotional and spiritual resources. This is embarrassing for sure, but I share it because I know as a fellow human, you can relate.

There is one thing we need to clarify here. Keep in mind, that we are trying to distinguish between actual tribe members who elevate us, and those people who occupy our mental space and drain our tribal battery. Those who drain us but don't serve us need to be eliminated from our Tribe.

I am also sharing this anecdote to illustrate another insight this exercise produces. Do the people you are investing your energetic resources in provide any real connection at all? Are they even in your actual world? If you find yourself with a lot of people who are not genuine connections, again you have some serious considerations to manage.

One of my favorite authors is Ryan Holiday. I have read all his books. Like me, he is into stoicism, and I often read his blogs and follow him daily on social media. I would like to add him in, but he is not an actual friend of mine and other than his work, I don't waste mental energy on him, so he is out. The woman I am dating is in.

Now, remember, I am not putting people into this grid who are acquaintances or people I kind of know unless, as stated, they are occupying my emotional resources in a significant way. Coworkers are not there. The cute barista I talk to every morning is not there either, although if I was crushing on her, stalking her FB page and feeling charged or drained by her she might be.

Get the point? These twenty people are individuals who impact you mentally, emotionally or spiritually. They are with you in your head—occupying energetic resources— daily or weekly. They are most often people you talk to or talk to you on a regular basis. They are people who have a piece of your energetic and emotional resources. They are people who you engage with and who engage with you. They could also be people you don't speak with at all if, and only if, they occupy a significant amount of mental or emotional energy.

Once you have your twenty individuals, you are ready to start filling in the grid.

Go down your list of individuals one by one, adding them into the grid in their proper place or places. Think about them as a whole. How do they make you feel? Do they support you? Do they bring positivity or negativity? Are they mixed— bringing benefits in one area and drawbacks in others?

Keep in mind that unlike most teams—where a player only occupies just one position—these players can maintain multiple positions. I will use my sister, Jodi, as an example. She is a support to me and is a solid member of my Tribe. She also is one of my greatest cheerleaders. She works for me and has become an integral part of my business and dream/mission. That makes her a Believer too. She can also act as Counselor. Emotionally she can hold space for me. So I would write her into the Tribe, Believer & Counselor areas of my grid.

So far so good.

Only one issue? Jodi is a total Enabler. I love to eat, and so she likes to feed me. I love wine, and she makes sure there is a horse-trough filled with it whenever I go over to her house. I mention I like these new Belgium butter cookies with chocolate molasses drizzle, and they are on my doorstep the next day.

I know it seems harsh, but I can't spend too much time over at my sister's house. If I asked her to go work out with me, I might wake up drunk in a vat of cream cheese in the back of an Italian pastry shop instead.

So, in addition to having her in the Tribe, Believer and Counselor areas of my grid, she would also be present in the Enabler block as well. In this way, Jodi occupies four areas in my Tribal battery. She is positive in three areas and negative in one. Understand the concept?

Now you have your grid filled with people. Some occupy

one spot, some many. Some may be in the same column; acting at times as a positive and at other times, a negative.

My business partner Gary is an example of this. He can act as a Believer sometimes and a Hater at other times. He has contrarian tendencies, and I have to be watchful when that comes out.

Your next step is to start making your assessments. The first thing you should do is take a look at the positive column compared to the negative column. Where do more people congregate? Do you have a Tribal Battery loaded with negatives, and no positives or the reverse? Any immediate insights?

Is your social battery as a whole draining or charging? This can tell you right away what is going on with your success and happiness.

I want to make one crucial point here. If you find yourself with more negatives than positives, you have to look at yourself and those who surround you carefully and make an honest assessment.

Before you assume someone else is the problem, you should ask the tough and obvious question—are you the issue?

One quick and easy way to determine if you are the issue, or if it's the other person, is to consider your patterns and theirs.

I have an ex-girlfriend who I felt like I did everything in my power to keep in my life as a friend. The two of us could not find balance and had a horrendous time with each other. My first rule is always to assume I am the problem.

Why would I do this? Because I know my nature as a human is to automatically assume the other person is to blame. This is called the "illusory superiority effect." It is a cognitive bias uncovered by social psychology researchers. Essentially, it tells us we will tend to overestimate our own intelligence, kindness and contributions and underestimate everyone else's. We will also underestimate our contributions to problems, while placing more of the blame on someone else. A Next Level Human is aware of this tendency, and works very hard not to fall for it. How can we grow as people if we see everyone else as the problem? Since I am the person trying to grow and get better, I am not served by blaming the other person, even if they deserve the bulk of the blame. This is a tactic some call "Extreme Ownership." If I want a thing to change, I first have to accept full responsibility for it, even when it is not my fault.

A mutual friend of my ex pointed something out to me. She said, "Jade, you are friends with almost all your exes. You and your ex-wife are closer than most friends I know. This ex, who you are trying so hard to keep as a friend, has broken relationships all over the place. I think your patterns and hers make it clear where the dysfunction lies."

I don't know about you, but I am terrified of being one of those people who everyone has an issue with, and I am the last to know. I want to grow and get better; that means looking at myself first and always.

In this case with my ex-girlfriend, I still could be the problem. Or, perhaps we both were the problem. However, our patterns and history do provide some clues. I rarely have issues with maintaining relationships; this particular ex historically has more than a few.

My favorite analogy to illustrate this point is bad breath. If you have bad breath there is no way to smell it— and no, blowing your breath into your cupped hand does not work. If you are using that technique, you are kidding yourself, my friend.

You can't smell your own breath, but everyone else can. And if you don't know you have bad breath, you want to be able to correct it, right? One solution is to assume the worst. This is a technique used by the stoic philosophers called "negative visualization." This is a practice where you assume what could go wrong, will go wrong, and by thinking about it, you are prepared. If you proactively assume your breath does stink, and as a result chew gum, brush your teeth, floss like crazy and suck on cloves, you are likely to never have to deal with the issue in the first place.

Social interactions are the same. By assuming you are the problem, rather than the reverse, you are giving the other person the benefit of the doubt and giving yourself a chance to grow and get better. As one of my favorite Stoic philosophers, Epictetus said, "It is impossible for a man to learn what he thinks he already knows."

But sometimes, it is not you. Sometimes the other person is the one with the bad breath, and you have to be honest about this.

After you assess whether your Tribal Battery is in a net negative or positive state, it is time to look at the individuals in more depth. Are they in more negative positions than positive ones? Are they, as an individual, a net negative or a net positive in your life? Are they, like my ex, either not interested in being a member of your Tribe or have dysfunctional tendencies you should consider?

Whereas before you could only guess at this; now you have a much more objective evaluation.

Finally, look at each box independently. Which are empty? Which areas are there only one or a few people? Where does your Tribe need positive reinforcement? Where is your team being hindered by a negative influencer? Where do you have superstars and where are your key players?

The usual reaction to completing this exercise is "WOW!!" Or "I had no idea." Or "No wonder."

You have just done a social accounting and full audit of

your Tribe. Now you are in a position of knowing. Now you can begin to take action.

As you wrap your head around the implications of your Tribal battery, immediate insights should surface.

In my case, I had one huge insight. I had no real Mentors in my life. I also realized there were some people who I was attached to, who had no net positive in my life. In fact, they were net negatives. They were acting as Vampires and Victims.

That is when I understood that I needed to make the hard cuts required, as well as draft some new players to my Tribe.

You are likely coming to some of the same realizations. You are also probably struggling with one big question. You may be thinking something like this, "Wow, I get it. This is great. But I have some people in my Tribe who are net negatives, and I simply can't avoid them."

This is normal, and one of the most important insights readers should gain from this exercise.

There is no doubt that there are people in your social circle who you will never be able to remove. In fact, some of them are loved ones and friends; stepchildren, parents, baby daddies, coworkers and others. How do you manage people who are net negatives but, for reasons beyond your control, cannot wholly be cut from the Tribe?

Below I have provided two examples of what this exercise might look like for me. It contains some real and fictitious people for the purposes of illustration. Below, in the first image, is a net positive tribal battery and represents something closer to my actual reality. The second image reflects a net negative Tribal Battery. See if you can pick out the areas in both scenarios I need to work on?

Where am I strong and where am I weak? Who is a net negative and who is a net positive?

Positive Tribal Battery

PEOPLE ↓	+	−
MOM	**TRIBE** — ELI KEONI JILL JILLIAN DANNY KIMO MOM DAD JANE GARY LAURA JODI	**EMPTY AUDIENCE**
DAD		
KEONI		
KIMO		
JILL	**BELIEVERS** — MOM DAD KEONI KIMO JODI	**HATERS** — KIMO KEVIN DAD ANN
JODI		
GARY		
ELI		
JILLIAN		
LAURA	**COUNSELORS** — MOM	**VAMPIRES** — BRENDA
DANNY		
RAY		
ANN		
KEVIN	**COACHES** — RONNIE RYAN RAY JILL KEONI GARY	**ENABLERS** — JODI KEVIN
RONNIE		
JANE		
BRENDA		
LISA	**MENTORS**	**VICTIMS** — LISA ANN
RYAN		

Negative Tribal Battery

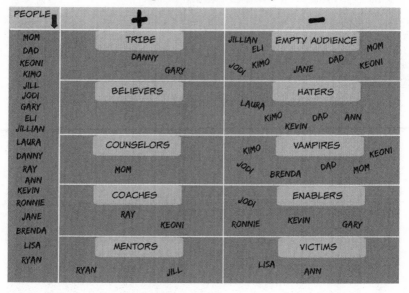

PEOPLE ↓	+	−
MOM	**TRIBE** — DANNY GARY	**EMPTY AUDIENCE** — JILLIAN ELI JODI KIMO JANE DAD MOM KEONI
DAD		
KEONI		
KIMO		
JILL	**BELIEVERS**	**HATERS** — LAURA KIMO DAD ANN KEVIN
JODI		
GARY		
ELI		
JILLIAN		
LAURA	**COUNSELORS** — MOM	**VAMPIRES** — KIMO KEONI JODI BRENDA DAD MOM
DANNY		
RAY		
ANN		
KEVIN	**COACHES** — RAY KEONI	**ENABLERS** — JODI RONNIE KEVIN GARY
RONNIE		
JANE		
BRENDA		
LISA	**MENTORS** — RYAN JILL	**VICTIMS** — LISA ANN
RYAN		

Let's go back to the sports analogy. In this case, you need to know when to use them in the game and when to take them out. You must discern how to offset their poor play by leaning on other players. And you should understand when to bench them entirely for a time. We will cover this in the tribe management chapter.

My coauthor, Danny is one of my closest friends and used to be my brother-in-law. We sometimes laugh at this weird co-nundrum of societal labels; what do you call the brother of your ex-wife? Danny and I are still best friends. I am also incredibly close to my ex-wife. I know it is a little strange, but we hang out one to two times per week and I am her go to babysitter for her adorable little Pomsky puppy named Pip. My relationship with Danny is a great one to illustrate the building of a Next Level Tribe. When I was married to Dan's sister, Jill, I had very few guy friends. Jill and I spent 24–7 together. We joke sometimes that the reason we split is because there is only a finite amount of time two people can be attached to each other. She and I spent 99% of our time together over the course of 10 years, probably more than any other couple in history. We worked from home together, traveled together, ate together, slept together, etc, etc.

It was, and still is, a great relationship but it illustrates the downside of not having a more diverse Tribe of people to lean on. Jill and I were everything to each other. We were coach, business consultant, lover, friend, wife/husband, workout part-ner, emotional support, and on and on. A healthy Tribe is a diverse Tribe.

Danny came to live with us for a period of three years after the trouble he had in college. It was amazing. He became my comic relief, my sounding board, my new workout partner, and filled several other gaps in my team that Jill filled. It was at this time that I realized I needed more Next Level Tribe members. He was the catalyst to helping me see I needed to cultivate more Next Level Relationships. Some of that was just about realizing I had great friends and family I was not leaning on. Some of it was about realizing I had gaps in my Tribal needs.

At that point I shuffled certain friends around to different positions in my Tribe. I started going to business conferences and met one of my best friends Dr. Ray Hinish, who has become a business coach and confidant. I went into business with my high school friend. I started working out again with an old workout partner. I hired a coach and a counselor for a time. I started building the Next Level Tribe I currently have.

This is the power of the Tribal battery exercise. It illuminates the weaknesses and strengths of your current social circle. But knowing who is on your Tribal team does not necessarily help you deal with all the the Tribal dynamics that can arise. We will cover that next in the tribal management chapter.

PART 4

• • •

Managing Your Tribe

By Jade Teta

"It's silly to try to escape other peoples' faults. They are inescapable. Just try to escape your own........ Leave other peoples' mistakes where they lie........ That kindness is invincible, provided it's sincere—not ironic or an act......"
—Marcus Aurelius—

Tribe Management

• • •

I had a friend I used to work with; let's call her Jane. She had a terrible relationship with her parents. I am not sure if they knew it or not, but I found out right away. Once I was hanging out with her at a coffee shop, and her phone rang. I looked, and it said, "Mom." She made a face and dismissed the call. At that time, I did not know her well enough to say anything, so I didn't.

Fast-forward into three months of working together and I witnessed this more than a handful of times. I asked her, "When was the last time you talked to your parents?"

"I talk to my dad all the time," she said. "But I don't talk to my mother or my stepdad."

She went on to explain to me that they were not supportive. They always asked her questions about what she was doing since she graduated. They expected her to take the GRE and she was supposed to be applying to a med school, but she was still trying to work out if that was indeed what she wanted to do, or if there was some other path she should take.

It had gotten so bad that she stopped talking to them altogether. This was strange to me since I had a great relationship with my family, even though we disagreed and yelled at each other all the time. That is what Italian families do.

Anyone who grew up around an Italian American family knows what I am talking about. Arguments start up quickly in our families. Once, I got into a fistfight with my two brothers over who was going to get the last slice of pizza.

We yell and scream at each other often, and then we cook a bunch of food, eat together, and all is well again. We don't talk about the argument of course, but the food is how we apologize and show love. In this case, my friend and her family were not communicating at all, not even in the slightly dysfunctional way that mine has a tendency to do. They also were not having any makeup feast. This was a very bad sign in my world.

After some time, we started to talk about it. She wanted a relationship with her mother and stepfather, but was adamant they needed to start treating her differently first.

She asked me my advice.

Stories We Tell Ourselves

Our perceptions of others and ourselves come down to stories. These stories are often written over an extended period, after silent and unconscious observations. These stories have some pretty insidious qualities. First, they are written in haste, during emotional times. And second, we are rarely even aware we are writing these stories.

Here is a simple case of how these stories come about using a non-social example. Take my disgust of spinach. The first time I had spinach as a little kid I put it in my mouth and immediately started to gag. My parents dumped the nasty stuff right out of the can, boiled the hell out of it, applied no salt, butter or flavor of any kind. When I took a bite, it was as if someone vomited green slime from their mouth into mine. I spit it out immediately. My mom and dad yelled at me as a result. In my house growing up, you were to eat what was put on your plate. My punishment was none of my favorite cheesy potatoes unless I ate my spinach.

From that day forward, I had an aversion to spinach. I still don't like the stuff. I also inexplicably become furious with my parents anytime anyone offers me anything green to eat. I am kidding about that last part, but this is not so far off from how we treat family members in regards to our childhood emotional traumas and wounds.

For example, my older brother Keoni used to tease me mercilessly as a child. I hated him for it. Then one day in our early twenties, I realized I was treating my brother as if he were still the eight-year-old brat that would tease me. How ridiculous is that?

Dynamics with family members are some of the toughest relationships in our lives because we humans don't like change. We want things neat and tidy. Your family loves that they know who you are— or think they do. They have a story about you and they are sticking to it. You also have a story about them and you are not going to give it up either.

Whether you want to accept it or not, your story is the problem. It has to be, because it is the only thing in this scenario you have the power to change, and change it you must. It is the only way you can hope to change their story as well.

There is one rule of social interaction that you need to understand. You should burn this insight into your psyche as if someone took a hot cattle iron to your forehead. That rule is this: **you can't change people**. Let me say that again, **you can't change people**.

People **can** change, but you can't change them. There is a way to entice people to change themselves, but in the end, whether they do is entirely up to them.

For my friend Jane to change her relationship with her parents, she had to change herself first. That meant changing the story she told herself about them.

Her story was they were not supportive of her. She needed to start seeing them differently before they would ever show up that way.

From my perspective, her parents seemed supportive. They paid for her college education. They called to check up on her. They paid for her to take the GRE. They seemed like they cared, but that was not how she saw it. For her part, Jane saw all this "support" as their way to control her, but her desire for a better relationship made her open to my coaching.

The first step of our plan was for Jane to start giving her parents the acknowledgement that she was craving from them. This goes back to the "always assume it is you" advice. That is the only way you will ever be able to make a difference in the outcome. When they called, she would say, "Thanks for calling guys, you are always so supportive."

She would own the relationship; take them out of the box she kept them in, by changing her story about them first. She would try to see their calling as not a way to control her, but as a way of trying to connect with her. With that shift in perspective, she would then acknowledge them for supporting her.

We also talked about the fact that she needed to be authentic and have firm boundaries with them. After all, she did not want to do this work if she had to pretend to be someone she wasn't. We couldn't rule out the idea that her parents had controlling tendencies entirely, but giving them the benefit of the doubt in this case was the best way to move forward.

So when she spoke to them, she did not blow smoke. When they were less than supportive she would say, "Well, I know you don't like it, but you have always been behind me, so I trust you will support me in this too."

In other words, she owned her choice and behavior entirely. I wondered if part of the issue was that she was not 100% clear on what she wanted to do with her life, so when her family inquired as to her plans, her own indecision and anxiety surrounding that huge decision flared up as a result.

Using these Tribal management strategies, she eventually chose where she was going in her career. She owned that. She also decided she would treat her parents as supportive until they gave her real, tangible evidence they were not.

She decided her course of action, and she chose to write a new story about her parents.

Of course, this could have gone two ways. There are two types of people in the world. If you say, "You are the best, I could not have done that without you," the first type will say, "Yeah, I know, you couldn't. It's lucky you have me."

The second type will say, "Don't be ridiculous, of course, you could. I am just glad to help."

If you say, "I am sorry it was my fault." The first type will say, "Yep, it is your fault - don't do it again."

The second type will say, "You know what, I am sorry too. I share in that responsibility."

The type of person you want in your life is the second type—the type that can meet you halfway. Flexible and open, they, like you, are more socially agile, or at least willing to attempt it.

Who Stays and Who Goes

I have one philosophy that particularly irks my immediate family: I don't think of family in the same way most people do.

There are blood relatives, and of course, they are family, uncles, cousins, and the rest. Some of these people are friends, and some of them are acquaintances. Others are people I don't care for at all.

The same applies to in-laws. Ok, so you married my brother or my sister? That makes you family by law, but are you really someone I want in my life, someone whose approval I seek?

Trust me, I know this is not a popular view in the world, but it is the way I have always seen it.

Because of this, I had to come up with a way of talking about family differently. To me there is family, and then there is Family; capital "F". Family is your Tribe, the people who you choose and the whole reason for this book. Sometimes they are blood relatives, and sometimes they are not.

As an example, my mother has a very large family —7 total siblings including her. On her side of my genetic tree, there are a lot of people who fall under the rubric of family, but I consider very few of them Family.

A social circle is an interesting dynamic. It is not one circle, but more like a series of concentric rings. Starting in the center closest to you is the inner circle, those are the people who are your Tribe. Those are the people you spend your most intimate time with and they are the Family you choose.

One level out is your close friends. You are tight with these people. You see them on the regular. You catch up for lunch or through an occasional direct message. You see them in your social media feed and leave a comment here and there. They are very close, but they are not your Tribe.

The next level out is acquaintances. These include coworkers, people you see at your child's sporting events, your neighbors, etc.

When you are working on social management in any one of these tiers, realize much of the tension comes from a difference of opinion on where your relationships lie.

Some people see me as their Tribe when I don't consider them mine. Some people I want in my Tribe, and they have no desire to be there. That is the way social interactions go.

The first thing you need to understand as you take ownership of your Tribe is to let go of those who are not fully committed and engaged in your relationship.

This is very much like having a superstar player on your sports team who is unhappy being there. You might get a lot out of them, you may love their energy, and they may charge you up, but they may not feel the same about you.

This is analogous to the general manager feeling like he or she has taken care of the player, but the star is feeling like he or she is being used or treated poorly.

I had a friend in high school and college. He wasn't a bad guy, but not someone I would have chosen for my inner circle. He seemed to love being around my friends and me, and that was fine. The only issue was that he was very competitive and had a real need for status. There was this undertone of negativity and competition frequently when he was around. When I graduated from college, I realized that the relationship was draining for me. I was always in a supportive coaching role, but I felt he was in competition with me.

I seemed to be a net positive for him while he was a net negative for me. At the time I did not have the maturity to manage things in a responsible, Next Level way. Instead, I was very

Base Level. I became distant, less responsive and indifferent. Eventually, he fell out of my circle entirely. I suppose it was necessary and healthy for me, and hopefully he reevaluated his competitive tendencies with friends, but for a long time, I lamented that I handled that situation in such an immature way.

Now, as a more mature and aware man, I handle things differently. I had a similar situation in the last few years. This friend wanted more time and attention than I could give. He would email, text, and call with questions about entrepreneurship constantly. I felt like I was being used for his career and networking goals. The next time he asked me about business, I said, "I have been feeling lately like I am emotionally tapped out. I need to spend time away from talking shop all of the time. When interacting with friends I want more lightness and fun and a two-way learning interaction." This happened a few more times and each time I reiterated the same thoughts in different ways. My actions were also more in line with what I wanted, less shoptalk and more fun. I was not accusatory, and I took responsibility for it. After all, I was the one obliging; it was up to me to set the new boundary. In response, he stopped calling, texting and emailing. It was a way for me to vet if he was someone that could be part of my Next Level Tribe. He had two options in response to me. First, he could just go away or become more distant. Second, he could start to contribute to charging my energetic battery by inviting me to hang, or talking about other, non-business related, things. He ended up becoming more distant. I would have won either way.

I also had a situation like this in reverse. Remember that ex-girlfriend who I wanted to remain good friends with? I am not entirely sure why she wanted to distance herself because she did not communicate with me. I was forced to watch her create distance between herself and me. She would ignore texts, not return calls and simply became less responsive. I would have loved the help in understanding how and why I was draining her, but sometimes that is not possible. My intuition told me it was a combination of old wounds, a new boyfriend, who likely did not want an ex as her friend, and a feeling of not having the emotional bandwidth to manage the type of open, honest friendship I desired.

This is an often-overlooked aspect of social dynamics. When it comes to your social circle, individuals have to want to be there. You can't recruit people in your Tribe who have no desire to be there.

As I cautioned before, if you find very few people want to be in your Tribe, then you can't rule yourself out as the problem. Either you need to give up investing time in people who don't invest in you, or you need to adjust your behavior to be more attractive to others. This is why the discussion of Danny's 3R model of Social Agility is so vital.

Self-awareness is one of the most critical aspects of being socially intelligent. Remember the bad breath example? If every time you talk to a friend, their eyes start watering, they keep their distance and offer you gum; you should take the hint.

By the same token, if it is just one person who offers you gum and is constantly backing away from your company, you can assume they are walking around with dog shit on their shoes and blaming the smell on you.

In the case of my friend Jane, she could not begin creating a new relationship with her parents until she fully understood these dynamics, and took time to examine the situation from all angles. Her parents needed to be on board for things to work out, and it turns out they were. They also wanted a relationship with their daughter. They were the type of people who had enough self-awareness to know they were part of the problem.

Here is the step-by-step on disconnecting with people who are a drain on your battery:

• <u>Self-awareness</u>: This comes first. Whenever you have an issue with someone, look to yourself first. Are they the problem or are you? Remember, social scientists tell us we suffer from the illusory superiority effect. This makes us always assume the other person is the problem. Resist this temptation by first assuming the issue is you. This is an example of what many refer to as "extreme ownership;" if it is an issue you want solved, you need to assume you are the one who must fix it.

• <u>Give the benefit of the doubt</u>: Let them out of the box. If you are stubbornly clinging to the way you view a person, even if they change, you won't notice it. Try seeing their behavior from a different perspective. Maybe they are not rude, but instead shy. When I was in college, my eyesight started to fail and I stubbornly waited until the last minute to do anything about it. A friend of mine told another friend I was rude because he waved to me several times on campus and I ignored him. Truth is, I could not see him to know he was waving. These kinds of assumptions often get us in trouble. Rather than jumping to conclusions, what if this person made the assumption I did not hear or see him instead?

• <u>Change the story</u>: If you want people to change, try providing them with a new way of seeing themselves. People have a funny tendency to live into the way they are seen by others. If you see them as lazy and they know it, they have all the incentive in the world to keep being that way. All humans have an intuitive sense that other people's perceptions of them are hard to change, so they just throw up their hands and say "the hell with it." Treat them differently, and see if they start being different as a result.

• <u>Vet their behavior</u>: Once you change the way you see them and treat them differently, you can see how they behave in response. Do they show up different or do they behave exactly the same? You have to give them a little time of course, but if they show up like they always did, it is time to consider cutting them from your Tribe.

• <u>Be Next Level</u>: A Next Level Human does not engage in Base Level avoidance and ghosting behavior, nor do they do Culture Level gossip and shit talk. To make it clear that you no longer have room in your Tribe, simply tell the truth. That truth almost always goes like this, "I am finding my emotional resources are drained so I am choosing to be less socially engaged in general, but more involved with my closest friends." I realize this sounds odd at first, but that is only because we are accustomed to not addressing these things head on. Part of that is because we almost never have to. Nine times out of ten, people pick up on the social signals and the distance is naturally created. In rare circumstances, this conversation needs to happen.

• <u>Know when to engage</u>: There are those who you will never be able to phase out of your Tribe completely. With these types, it is about defining clear boundaries. In terms of my family, I simply stopped talking about business with them. I would halt any conversation that went in that direction and say, "I realize you would do things differently, but what I require is support and belief. You are great in those areas in other ways, but in this case we don't see things the same, so let's talk about something else." This is easier than you think as long as you don't go Base Level. A Next Level Human is going to give love and affirmation in other areas rather than just shut someone down. Say something like, "Look you guys are amazingly supportive and I know you have my back if I need it, but in this case I prefer to do things my way."

Me, You, and Ume

In every relationship, there are three entities. Two of these entities are real people, and the other is formed from the dynamics of the relationship.

Let's say you and I are friends. In that relationship there is me, there is you, and then there is the third entity of me plus you. Let's give this third entity a name to make it more tangible. Let's call it the you/me or Ume.

Relationships start going sideways when Ume begins to dominate over either you or me. Relationships also tilt in an unhealthy direction when either you or me start to value Ume more than we appreciate the other person in the relationship.

From a romantic perspective, this might be someone who feels that all your extra energy should go into Ume. They may not like that you are cultivating other separate relationships with the girlfriends you go shopping with or the brothers you drink and shoot pool with. A smart, Next Level Human is going to support other relationships that charge up their romantic partner. They understand that the growth and stimulation of other relationships will eventually help the Ume of their romance thrive and be strong.

This is exactly the same for friendships. Think of a friend who hangs out with another group of friends where they have their own separate Ume dynamics. Those relationships strengthen their personal energy bank and allow them to bring more to the relationship with you.

These dynamics occur in romantic relationships in other obvious ways, but that is another book, and it happens in other types of relationships as well.

The best relationships feed off of Ume in a way that sustains both parties. Ume should support and bolster you and me, not the other way around. A good relationship should increase the energetic resources of both, not drain them.

Sometimes I will pull a little more energy out of Ume, maybe if I am going through a tough time while you will give a bit more energy to Ume, shouldering the burden. And, of course, you will need to pull energy out of Ume at times while I sustain Ume with a little more of my energetic reserves. If all goes well, Ume becomes a separate energetic reservoir for us both. It is like having a third friend we can both rely on in times of need.

This ebb and flow of natural balance between you, me, and Ume is what is meant by give and take. It is the energetic savings account of the relationship.

The critical point is that over time, the distribution of energetic resources needs to equal out. That is what can be beautiful about a great friendship. The energy of Ume can, at times, be expansive and self-generating. When that happens, we both benefit immensely from it.

This balance starts to break down when one person is investing a lot of energy into Ume while the other is continuously drawing energy from Ume. This is an all too frequent and familiar occurrence, and it exposes the complicated nature of this sort of close relationship.

Many people are natural givers. They built their entire self-perception on the idea that good people give and are selfless.

It's a beautiful thought, but it comes with a potentially serious downside. Not everyone is selfless in their reciprocity style. In fact, some people are the opposite. When a selfless giver gets into a relationship with a selfish taker, the giver can be sucked dry.

In his book, *Give & Take*, Adam Grant highlights the upsides and downsides of being a giver. What he uncovered in his research is that Givers fare the worst of any other social management style. He also found Givers faired the best.

I know this sounds contradictory; so let me explain.

The difference between healthy Givers, who succeeded in their relationships versus those unhealthy Givers, who had difficulties, was that those who understood the Ume dynamic were able to maintain strong Tribal battery charges. Those Givers who weren't aware of the balance of the Ume drained their batteries because they gave and gave without getting anything back from Ume.

The healthy givers gave generously, but also stayed tuned into the social energy dynamics of their relationships. If the other person was always pulling energy out of Ume, while the Givers were always putting energy in, the Givers changed their tribal management style. Instead of remaining Givers, they became Matchers.

This is precisely the dynamic we all need to become very sensitive to.

When managing the Ume of your relationships, you need to realize that people fall into three basic categories: there are

Givers, there are Takers, and there are Matchers. In psychology research, we call these reciprocity styles.

A Giver who always gives will often attract Takers who always take. Think about it. Why would a Taker who always gets what they want ever have reason to change? They have their energy fed and will continue to enjoy that situation as long as the Giver allows it. The Taker will stay fat and happy while the Giver starves.

There is only one way to deal with a Taker: become a Matcher. Once you become a Matcher, the Taker has no choice but to meet you halfway or starve themselves. This is what healthy, successful Givers do. They still give, but they are careful about how much and to whom.

The ability to switch reciprocity styles like this is essential. It is also another perfect vetting strategy for your relationships.

Let's go back to my friend, Jane, and her parents. She started out as a Matcher with her parents and then switched to being a Giver. This was the only viable first move for her. It was a good step because someone needed to attend to Ume and infuse it with some energy. If she wanted to repair the relationship, she needed to assume she was the problem and take full responsibility for it first.

At the same time, Jane needed to be very careful and watch to see if her parents met her halfway. Would they also start to pour energy into Ume when they felt her effort and energy? This is what began to happen. Her parents also switched into a more giving role. It resulted in a positive change and a relationship that became sustaining and enriching for both parties.

What if they did not start feeding Ume energy? What if they became Takers or remained Matchers, ignoring her attempts at positivity and effort to connect, and instead viewed her careful approach as weakness? At that point, the dynamics of the relationship would need to be adjusted once again. Not speaking at all is not healthy, so there is another way: setting clear boundaries around the relationship.

Had Jane not taken the first step she would not have been able to fully vet the relationship and there would have been no forward momentum. Instead of withdrawing all energy from Ume out of frustration and impatience, she decided to put her energy back in. If her parents had not adjusted, she would have needed to switch back to being a Matcher. Becoming a Matcher is synonymous with developing boundaries.

Owning Yourself

There is one thing that has to come first before setting boundaries, and that is being Real. You need to know where you stand and be your authentic self. Once you do this, you can manage your Tribal dynamics, and you can easily identify imbalances in Ume.

Have you ever heard of the law of attraction? You know, the idea that you sit down, take some deep breaths, say Ohmmmmm a few times and then wish upon a star— by thinking what you want—and it eventually happens? By this logic, if you want a fantastic, beautiful, romantic partner, you think about it a lot, and he or she will show up.

Sounds like fairytale stuff, right? Well, it is. The "law of attraction" is not real and is not something you can use in the real world. There is, however, a "law" that is real and can be used: "the law of recognition."

Let's say you decide you are going to buy a Tesla. You had not thought about the Tesla before, but now you have researched it and are contemplating getting one. You think you may want one in red. Now you start noticing Teslas, don't you? As if by magic they are everywhere, and inexplicably, a high percentage of them are red.

This is not the law of attraction; it's the law of recognition. When you start thinking about and researching the Tesla, you are priming your brain to recognize them. Those Teslas— yes, even the red ones—were there the whole time. You did not call them into existence; you started to be aware of what was already around you.

This is how authenticity works too. Once you decide to own yourself completely, you immediately become visible to all the people who have been looking for that type of person. The way you carry yourself and the confidence you project will send a message to those around you. You'll start recognizing the people you are looking for as well. This is the first stage of creating a Next Level Tribe that will consist of longtime friends, and some new ones too. This is tribal management 101.

Most of us go about this the wrong way. You will have to follow me closely here, because I may seem to be contradicting myself from what I said above. Remember when I said that when you are fully occupying your authentic self, others recognize you, and you recognize them? Well, this process takes time. Being real takes guts and requires you weather the initial storm of doubt that will come your way. People you have never met may immediately get it, but your current Tribe members may have some initial doubt. Can you blame them?

Let's say you decide you are going to become the next great American cupcake maker. This is who you really are, what you really love, and what you are genuinely committed to. But you can't expect that people will immediately start treating you that way.

It just doesn't work like that. They will eventually see you as exactly that, but authenticity needs to be proven; initially to yourself, and then to others. We humans need to learn to see ourselves the way we wish to be perceived, and that can take some time. In fact, the initial skepticism we may encounter is part of the process. It is as if life is saying, "It is easy to be real to yourself. It is easy to be motivated when no one is watching. It is easy to be all-good when everything is all-good. Before you are going to be completely recognized by others, you need to prove it; this requires a process of confidently moving forward when no one else believes but you." Then guess what happens? Everyone else starts to see you that way too.

Before anyone else sees the amazing pastry chef you know you are, you have to start showing up every day with flour on your apron. You need to see yourself churning out delicious icings. Even then, you will encounter mostly Haters and Vampires.

But, the more you show up as you, the more you will become visible to those around you, and the more they will be recognizable to you. The more they see you, the more they get you. More importantly, the more you will start to see yourself the way you want to be seen too.

Jane wanted to make money in the fitness industry and start an online business. Her parent's response to that was, "Oh, so you are giving up medical school and want to be a PE teacher?" Although Jane did not see being a PE teacher as a bad choice of profession, her parents did.

This type of response can be damaging to even the most confident person. But by that time, Jane knew better. She could see through this because she knew what was happening.

What was going on was that her parents were in the Hater side of her Tribal Battery. The good news is she had other

Believers on her side. By owning who she was, what she was going to do, and then taking full responsibility for managing her Tribal Battery— and her dynamic with her parents— they had no choice but to become Believers too.

This is what is possible once you understand the Tribal Battery, the Tribe dynamic, and Tribal management styles.

But what happens when someone does not change? What happens if they stay Haters? What happens if they are a net negative, but you have no choice about whether they stay on your Tribal team or not?

First, you do have a choice. You are in charge of who stays and who goes. You must take full responsibility for the management of your Tribe.

I will again use my family as an example here. I am a lucky guy. My immediate family members have always been Believers and Tribe members. But there are certain areas where the Tribe dynamics of Ume break down even with them.

Let's imagine you are a part of a hunter-gatherer tribe. Let's say your Tribe has a star hunter. They are your go-to-guy or girl to help feed everyone. You lean on them heavily for that job. Now, let's say you need someone to stay at the camp and help a sick member of the Tribe. Are you going to use your best hunter for that job? Of course not, hunters are not good at healing and without them on the hunt, no one gets fed. You need to call in your master herbalist instead.

My older siblings have always been supportive believers in me. That being said, they also fall into the Victim or Enabler categories in certain situations.

This adds another wrinkle, but the hunter-gatherer example will continue to illustrate. In a Paleolithic Tribe like this, if you are at war with another Tribe, you have a group of people you call on for that job, the warriors. When you are in the middle of a famine, you have another set of people that you lean on, the hunters. The "players on the field" change, based on what the circumstances dictate. If winter is coming and you have plenty of food, but no warm clothing, you mobilize the skinners and fur makers.

I realized this while working with my family. My older brother, Keoni, and I, started a natural medicine clinic with our family. My other brother, Kimo, and my sister, were net positives on my Tribe in this scenario. My sister, Jodi, was a Coach when I was in the clinic. She worked the front desk, made sure I had a break for lunch and would keep me fed and focused. Kimo helped with buying initial supplies for the clinic and acted as a Believer. Keoni, who worked with me in the clinic, acted as a Mentor by exposing me to new ideas and keeping me up-to-date on some of the research he was reading in herbal medicine.

Once I started to branch out into being an Internet entrepreneur, the dynamics changed a bit. Jodi and Kimo, who had some business background, began to become Victims. They peppered me with constant opinions of what I was doing right and what I was doing wrong. To them anything that was not their idea was a bad idea.

When things went right they would say, "I told you so!" When things went wrong, they would say, "I warned you about that; you never listen." For a while I was running around like crazy, listening to everything they said and trusting their judgment instead of my own. Things were a disaster. I was drained, and our relationship as a whole was suffering.

Finally, I had to realize that they could not be effective members of my Tribe in this area of my life, so I stopped listening to them and started doing my own thing. I figured if I fail or succeed I would need to do it on my own. I set out to find different Mentors, Believers and Coaches who could support me in my new endeavors.

When my siblings became less supportive, they moved from Tribe members to an Empty Audience and emotional Vampire status. They were watching me and talking to me, but not helping or supporting. In fact, they were draining me.

In one social dynamic they were net positives, and in the other, they were heading net negative. I had to set boundaries and eventually stopped speaking to them about business at all.

How did I know they were the issue and not me? Over time, I gathered enough experience with other people to know my relationship style in this regard was fine. I also saw them repeating the same patterns with my brother, Keoni, and each other, as well as others. In time I saw I was not the problem, but I was still responsible for managing it.

In this example, to make sure my assessment of my siblings was accurate, I had to look at their business patterns compared to my own. I then needed to correct any of my dysfunctions and erect boundaries against theirs. In this case, I did a little of both.

Don't get me wrong, I love my siblings, and I know any of them would take a bullet for me. But when it came to talking business, I knew they were not productive people for me to discuss my plans with. It took time, but I had to establish clear boundaries. When I needed to bounce business ideas off of someone, I chose another friend to connect with. When I was with my siblings, I steered the conversations into topics that worked for everyone. When I did, my energy reserves grew, and my business improved as did my relationships with my siblings.

Here is another example: let's say I am stressed about money.

I know not to go to my mother about this issue. She is likely to be an Enabler in this sense and say, "Oh, don't worry honey, money comes and goes. You will be fine."

Instead, I would go to my Dad in this case. I know from past situations he would offer sound advice, and counsel me in a way Mom could not.

If I wanted to do a real-estate deal, I would approach my two brothers who could offer real counsel in this regard. If I needed support building a start-up Internet business, they would be the last people I would go to. They would be net negatives in that regard.

One of the big mistakes people make is expecting one person to play all the positions on their team. This happens in romantic relationships where a lover is expected to be the quarterback, the kicker, the linebacker and the water boy. That kind of social management is untenable.

Tribal management is first, and foremost, your responsibility. People do change, but you can't force that change on them; instead you have to own yourself, and reframe your relationship. Open yourself to changing the story you are telling about them before they ever start to see you differently. It's important to revisit how we categorize and put friends into boxes, sometimes without even realizing it, and be open to adjusting those judgments.

Building Boundaries and Tearing Them Down Again

To keep from making the mistake of being overly rigid with people who drain your Tribal Battery, you can practice a generous social management style when setting and evaluating boundaries in your life. In a relationship where you are forced to become a Matcher you can, every once in a while, be selfless and generous to see if the other person has changed. If they have adjusted, you may find that they match you back instead of taking from you.

Let's say you are one of those people who naturally enjoys treating when eating out with friends. It is your automatic default, something you do often without thinking. Next Level Humans often do these things instinctually, without much thought. But let's say after about the twentieth time, you notice your friend NEVER offers to pick up the tab or is slow on the draw when the bill comes. As a result, you go from a Giver to a Matcher. However, you are still a giver at heart so every once in a while, you pick up the tab even with your Taker friend. This allows you to get joy from giving, and also determine if they have altered their reciprocity style. If they have, rather than letting you pay, they will insist you split the check. You may even find they offer to pick it up instead. This "generous matching" style is a good middle ground for those who get joy from giving, but also don't want to be taken advantage of by a Taker.

It is important to remember life is happening to us all the time. Life is one huge biofeedback machine. While you are out in the world interacting with people, learning about yourself and adjusting accordingly, so are others. If you want others to change, you need to be willing to take them out of the box you placed them in, at least long enough to give them a chance.

I went through near bankruptcy, an affair, a betrayal, divorce, and all the rest. I had immense positive change as a result of it all. I am not anything like the guy I was then. My relationships are not either.

There is another way I assess people in my social circle. If a member of my Tribe continues to see me a way I am not, or no longer wish to be, it is up to me to help them upgrade their position in my Tribe, or cut them all together.

Boundaries are the vital component here. To establish meaningful and effective boundaries, you need to have all the elements I talked about in place: self-awareness, authenticity, extreme ownership, insight into the Ume dynamic, and the ability to recruit the right team members at the right time, and for the right situation.

Here is a final example of how this entire process comes together. Let's use your significant other in this case.

Let's say your significant other never does their dishes. You have asked them to do their part of this chore multiple times. You have explained that the distraction of the dishes not being done drains you and makes you less productive in other areas.

They still don't do their dishes.

The usual approach would be to badger them about the dishes. "Why don't you do the dishes? You never do the dishes. Any time there are dishes you always leave them for me." Sometimes this sort of nagging can escalate and become, "You never do anything around here to help! You are useless," which you really don't want to happen.

This approach doesn't work because you are repeating and reinforcing a story you don't want. If you continue telling them the story that they are not good at doing dishes, it is only natural that they will continue to live into that story.

I call this the "What the Hell Effect." If you let a human know that you have placed them in a box, they often—usually unconsciously—keep right on behaving that same way.

You know as well as I do that there is nothing more frustrating than someone putting you in a box and not letting you get out. Most humans react to this type of situation by throwing up their hands and saying, "What the hell. There is no use in changing. They will never see me differently anyway."

The critical step is to change your story about them first. This is a much better way of motivating them, unconsciously, to change their behavior. As long as they hear they are not doing the dishes, what incentive do they have to do the dishes?

This is psychological slight-of-hand, and it works. Do your best to see them as someone who does do their share of the dishes. If you see them pick up a cup and move it even two inches closer to the sink, you say, "Oh wow. Thanks for helping with the dishes. I love it when you help with the dishes."

Or you start noticing them helping in other ways. "Oh, wow. Thanks for always helping me. You are great."

Once you establish the new story of them as "helper," and you share that with them, you wait and watch. Which type of person will now show up?

Are they the type of person who says, "Yeah, I actually do the dishes all the time and you are welcome," while continuing not to do the dishes? Or are they the type of person who says, "I know you like the dishes done and I am trying to be better. Thanks for noticing."

If they are the latter, congratulations on your social agility skills. If they are the former, it is time to make a serious accounting of the Ume dynamic.

Once you see they are not going to change, you should begin to move from a Giver to a Matcher.

While this tactic might sound a bit manipulative and sneaky, it's really not as bad as you might think. When I was 24 and my niece, Alisa, was 7, I babysat for her and my 6-month old nephew, Quentin, for a week. Don't even ask why I was tasked with this. I mean, who leaves their infant son and 7-year old daughter with a twenty-year-old dude for a week? I have teased my brother and sister-in-law about this ever since.

The first day Alisa made a horrible mess, I asked her to clean it up, and she said no. The next day I told her what a good helper she was whenever I could find even the slightest shred of evidence. This did not help; Alisa continued making messes, and not cleaning them up.

Then I switched things up. She asked me to go to her favorite fast food restaurant, and I said, "No, I can't. Someone needs to clean up your messes. If you start cleaning up after yourself, I will take you."

She didn't clean up the messes.

Later she asked again if I could take her to eat. I said, "No. I am sorry I need you to do some things for me first. If you clean up your mess, I have no problem taking you."

She still did not clean up her mess.

Eventually, when she was starving, she asked once again if we could get something to eat. I still said no. Finally, she cleaned up her mess, and I took her to eat.

By being firm, communicating my boundaries and explaining my expectations, she got the picture. I did not need to yell and scream and make a fuss. I just needed to let Alisa's messes pile up and communicate the consequences of her leaving those messes. She could leave them if she wanted - that was up to her. I purposely let them pile up around her. If she wanted me to meet her halfway, she needed to take the steps necessary to make that happen.

This worked because I saw what would happen all week if I kept cleaning up her messes and doing whatever she wanted. She would continue to take advantage of me.

Once I saw how it was going to be, I switched my reciprocity style to one of a Matcher. I let her know my expectations, and I stuck to my guns. I did not keep her in the dark. She knew what was required. I then left it up to her.

And, because I did not want to keep her stuck in a box she could never escape from, every once in a while I did clean up her mess asking nothing in return. This was my way of assessing if she was changing from Taker to Matcher. In fact, she was.

By the end of the week, we were both helping each other clean, working as partners to take care of her brother, and getting along great.

Yes, she was a child, and I was an adult, but the same dynamics are at play no matter the age of the person you are dealing with. All you need to do is know yourself, be willing to tell a different story about the people you are hoping will change, and be crystal clear in your communications, boundaries, and actions.

This social management system rarely fails. We fail to use it because we get stuck in expectations, assumptions, stories, and bad behaviors. I can say with certainty that the only time this system does not work is when we humans fail to use it.

PART 5

• • •

Lies, Gossip & Communication

By Jade Teta

*"Keep it a hundred, I'd rather you
trust me than to love me"*
—Kendrick Lamar—

Being a Next-Level Friend

• • •

Connection is a tricky thing. Creating your Next Level Tribe is not just about learning the 3Rs, managing your Tribe, and charging your Tribal Battery. It is also about being a better friend yourself. In fact, that is what it's about first and foremost.

You have to be a Next Level Person in order for those types of people to show up for you. You need to be a superstar Tribe member yourself. That involves being aware of how you talk about your friends, and is why we have to discuss the topic of gossip.

Talking about Others

"I can't believe you are sitting around talking shit about me!"

"What?" I said. "I'd never do that. I was sticking up for you. I would never let someone disparage you. Anytime I've heard anyone say something about you, I've come to your defense."

This was one of those *Twilight Zone* moments with a friend. She had just gone through a divorce where she was caught having an affair. I was telling her something I heard, and she was lashing out at me. She immediately jumped to the conclusion that I was taking part in a gossiping session about her.

As someone who was close to her, seeing her go through this life-changing ordeal was agonizing to watch. There were a lot of unpleasant things being said about her in our circle of mutual friends. The Haters in her life had magnified 10-fold as a result of what happened. People like her are an easy target. She is a confident and charismatic person and one of those people that others often love to hate. I have observed that confidence like hers is inspiring to other confident people, but simultaneously threatens insecure people.

I could understand she was extra sensitive, but how in the world could she see me as an enemy? Especially when I had proven I had her back over and over again. I was there for her financially, helped her out with a job and checked in with her constantly. I was concerned and doing my best to look out for her. I adamantly defended her, and her new boyfriend, whenever I heard anyone say anything negative. But, in one short little sentence, I saw clearly what I had started to suspect. She no longer trusted me.

"Wow," I thought. I was very much hurt by the fact she saw me like all the other backstabbers.

That was my initial reaction, but after a few days—after I considered the situation further and checked my assumptions— it made sense. My friend had been through a lot. I had seen her do her fair share of negative talk on many occasions. Of course, someone who says negative things about others is going to assume others are talking bad about them, right?

I watched this play out in my own family. Aside from my father, everyone got a huge kick out of talking about all the shortcomings of whatever family member was not in the room.

I grew up with this type of gossip. It was standard family procedure. It would involve stuff about how an in-law never cleaned up after herself or how someone else in the family was getting fat or how another person was clueless with money. I never thought much of it until I spent a five-year period watching this kind of gossip escalate into something that nearly destroyed the relationships of my siblings. You know the expression, "Never go into business with family." My family did not heed that warning. The truth is; it was not the going into business together that was the problem; it was the lack of communication; not speaking about concerns directly to each other's faces, and the prevalence of too much talk behind one another's back. My brother, Keoni, and I had successfully started and built a lucrative clinic together. It worked because we were in constant communication and learned from living together for six years in medical school how to manage. That took a lot of growing pains on both of our parts, but the practice paid off.

At the time all this family drama was going down, I was becoming more aware of my own tendency towards gossip in the past. It is hard to resist this behavior when it is a habit embedded and reinforced in your Tribe. After observing the fast deterioration of my family dynamics, I developed a severe distaste for gossip and vowed to work diligently to never engage in it. It now makes me viscerally disgusted when I watch others shit-talking behind people's backs.

However, talking about other people is something that is a natural consequence of being human. We are relational creatures and we use discussions of others to reality check ourselves and to bond.

To Gossip or Not to Gossip?

Research shows two-thirds of our conversations are about other people not in the room. The other third centers on weather, politics, sports, TV shows, etc.

We all like to gossip, but none of us wants it done to us. Typical humans, right?

Research states that those who gossip the most are the least liked and least trusted among their friends. These gossipy individuals believe others less as well, and are more paranoid as a whole.

At the same time, talking about others has had a huge role in human evolution and civilization. It is one of the ways we build trust. We tend to share our thoughts about others only with people we feel close to.

Gossip has an upside and a downside. The trick is to know how to use it.

Why We Gossip

The original purpose of gossip has to do with early human social structures. We first evolved in small bands of people and survival depended on the group getting along, doing the right thing, and working together. The primary threats to survival were being able to find food and avoiding becoming food. Groups made us more successful in both endeavors, but also required that we gave up some of our individual needs in favor of the group dynamic. Gossip served a vital role within these tribes to help members understand who the leaders were, who was pulling their weight, and who was freeloading or cheating the collective.

Let's say you are stuck in a wilderness setting with ten other people and have no better prospects or ability to strike out on your own. You must rely on each other.

You go on hunts, you collect berries, you build shelters, and you talk a lot. A natural consequence is that you will develop a relationship with everyone in your group. Although naturally, you will be closer to some than others.

There will be a lot of talking between individuals, within smaller groups, and in the main group. Most of what's discussed is who is doing what.

You may notice that on the last hunt Bob stayed in the back and did not fully take part. You share this with someone in the group. They tell you that he also seems to be taking the biggest portions at dinner. You learn from someone else that Bob seems to like to take long naps during the day and does not gather much firewood. And the last time the hyenas attacked, Bob was nowhere to be found.

Soon, everyone in the group gets the word that Bob is a "freeloader." That does not sit well with the group. If all works correctly, Bob should pick up on the fact that he is being looked down upon. His need to fit in, not just to save face socially, but also in order to survive will cause him to correct his behavior. If he does not alter his actions, the group leaders will intervene and set him straight.

This is how gossip functioned in its early days and, in many ways, this same mechanism is at work in today's cultures as much as it was back then.

Next Level Gossip. Good, Authentic Communication (GAC)

Gossip may have been helpful in the past and can be beneficial today, but we must distinguish between the different types of gossip. Negative gossip is the type that disparages people (i.e. "talking shit"). Harmless gossip is the kind that provides constructive feedback so people can learn and become positive, productive members of the group. Then there is gossip that sort of sits in the middle and can be destructive or useful depending on the circumstances.

I see these three types of gossip on a continuum from harmless and perhaps even beneficial, to neutral and then destructive and detrimental. In order to help categorize gossip appropriately, I use three separate words for it; Chatting, Dishing & Shit Talking. Chatting is harmless and can even be positive and productive; Dishing is more neutral. Shit Talking is negative. Chatting is respectful and focused on the person talking, like this: "Mary said 'X', and it got me to thinking. Can I get your opinion?"

Dishing is more detail oriented, like "I heard Mary got divorced. What happened? She seems to always have issues with people."

Shit Talking is malicious in intent and attacking in nature. "Mary is rude as hell, never picks up the tab and I heard so-and-so say she cheated on her husband."

This illustrates how gossip can range from relatively benign to obviously ill intentioned. Sometimes it can be difficult to tell since gossip is often unconscious and habitual for those who do it. One way to distinguish is to ask yourself if the gossip is overtly or subtly designed to empower the person doing the gossip while simultaneously degrading the reputation of the person being gossiped about.

With Chatting, it is usually very clear no one is being disparaged. Dishing can be harmless as well, but often has an undertone of self-righteousness attached. Shit Talking is meant to directly damage the reputation of the other person.

We can think of talking shit as the least evolved, more

destructive and Base Level form of gossip. In this form, you are not trying to help anyone. The purpose is to attack in the most cowardly way, when the person or people can't defend themselves. As a Base Level behavior, this type of gossip is all about degrading the other person in a way that positions the gossiper as a winner and the person they are talking about as the loser. With Dishing, it can go either way, but it most often has Culture Level motivations behind it. You may be bored, have nothing else to talk about, or you are self-righteous and stirring up drama. All of that is intended to make you look good and get other people on your team, while making the other person look bad and trying to get people off of their team.

We all know people like this. Given we are all human, we have all fallen prey to temptation in our basest and most petty moments, and likely engaged in these more negative styles of gossip ourselves at some time or another.

So how do we keep our gossip more Next Level? What does that even look like?

I call it Good Authentic Communication, or GAC for short. This type of gossip has a different intent. The goal is to either clarify a point or communicate and help, versus being haughty, self-righteous or stirring things up.

It is pretty easy to distinguish between the two. You only need to live by one rule. That rule is: Never say anything behind someone's back that you would not confidently say in the same way to their face.

This one rule immediately helps you distinguish Base Level gossip—i.e., Shit Talking —from Next Level gossip, or GAC. When you live this rule completely, other people will soon come to see you as a straight shooter who does not talk behind people's back. And like we talked about previously, when you go

Next Level, it helps other Next Level people recognize you as a like-minded person they can form close, trusting bonds with. These people may end up being some of the closest members of your Next Level Tribe.

I know that giving up gossip cold turkey is a hard pill to swallow and is far easier said than done for most. Our own need to be liked often precludes us from giving anyone negative feedback to their face. To get around this, we discuss the negative traits of these people with other people. But, if we are going to commit to having better, more effective relationships, it's critical we find a better way.

Here is a humorous example to illustrate good gossip from bad. Let's say a mother and daughter are gossips. They like to talk about all the drama in the family. It is how they bond, but it is also how the entire family learned about Uncle Mike's second hemorrhoid surgery.

Most of the time they are just Chatting. It's harmless and it helps them and everyone else catch up on family affairs. They rarely Shit Talk, because they are not cruel or malicious. However, they frequently crossover into Dishing, and this is where things go wrong.

Talking about the uncle's hemorrhoids is an example. Few people want their rectum to be the topic of conversation at a family gathering. The uncle finds out the health of his sphincter has been the subject of conversation after several family members ask him if he would like an extra pillow on his chair while trying to contain their laughter.

This may seem funny, and it is, if you are not the one whose butt was assaulted by a razor blade; but to Uncle Mike, it is embarrassing and hurtful. His sister was the only one he told, and now the entire family knows. He lets it go. She never knows how it impacted him, but Mike also never confides in his sister again, even in trivial matters. The episode eroded trust and slowly created distance between sister and brother. The other family members will also know not to entrust the mother and daughter with anything they don't want to get out either. This may seem like a small thing, but this type of negative gossip can cause serious harm in families, and with friends.

How do you know if the gossip is negative or positive? Before discussing other people's business ask yourself two questions. First ask, "Would I be comfortable if it were me and someone told others about this?" Next ask, "Would I feel confident saying this about the person if they were listening?"

The example above is negative gossip because it is an embarrassing and touchy subject that the uncle chose not to share openly with the family. It would not be negative gossip if the uncle had already mentioned the surgery to several other people in the family.

Self-Verification and Self-Enhancement
You probably think that people have a natural tendency to want to hear nice things about themselves. Research shows this to be true—it's called self-enhancement theory.

What you may not know is that people have a stronger drive for self-verification. Self-verification is the need to hear what we believe is true about ourselves.

We all view ourselves in a particular way. What research shows is that we trust other's evaluations of us more when they give us feedback that matches our self-perceptions. This is more important to us than positive feedback.

Being liked vs. Being honest
So, we like it when people say nice things about us, but we won't trust the person if we feel their perception of us is way off. If

they don't see us the same way we see ourselves, we may think that person is full of shit and not very genuine. If you want a Next Level connection with people, you need to know how to walk this fine line.

I know it seems I am telling you two conflicting things— say nice things but, at the same time, be honest about what you see. But what I am trying to communicate is that humans value authenticity and truth over placating and blowing smoke. We want honest feedback.

When we get genuine feedback, we begin to feel more comfortable providing our honest assessments back to others, opening up a productive two-way connection. If everyone was committed to this type of communication, fewer people would be in the dark as to why they feel alienated socially.

Scaled up, putting this into practice would be like the Yelp reviews for personal development. Get negative feedback from a few people, and you can dismiss it as opinion, and it might be. Get the same feedback again and again and again, and you have a pretty solid understanding of who you are in the eyes of others. That gives you the ability to make some positive changes in your life.

Shit Talking keeps potentially helpful insights hidden away and fosters distrust among everyone. People who engage in harmful gossip are not trusted. We know that if they are doing it to others, they are doing it to us too.

This may be why research shows we all have 50% fewer friends than we think we do. Your so-called "friends" often don't consider you a friend in the same way. Part of this is a consequence of all the negative gossip we engage in. If someone hears you talk shit about other people you call "friends," they assume you are doing the same to them.

This is a sad thing if you ask me. Don't you want to know your friends see you as a friend too?

This is why that rule about never saying anything behind a person's back you would not feel confident saying to their face is important. When you come at it from this point of view, your language becomes more empathetic and less judgmental. You are less self-righteous and more compassionate, and the gossip automatically moves towards the harmless Chatting type and not the negative Shit Talking type.

Another useful tool when talking about others is to simply qualify what you are saying. Make it clear to everyone that you are only telling one side of the story, your side. Say, "If Bob were here, he might disagree with this. He may have a different take. This is my view." Or say, "This is my opinion and the way I see it. I could be wrong."

This helps in not disparaging friends who are not present. It also tells the friends who are listening that you are trustworthy and respectful.

How To Manage Feedback

In person, your language is more conciliatory, empathetic and compassionate. But you must always speak your truth. Your goal is not to hurt someone's feelings, but sometimes that is unavoidable.

You should never hold back your truth to spare someone's feelings. Doing so serves no one and makes for dishonest relationships over the long term.

At the same time, if you really want to enhance, rather than degrade a friendship, you need to tread carefully. Giving someone feedback can backfire. This has been understood in psychology research for over 20 years. Feedback in one study resulted in a 40% decline in performance at work.

The same seems to apply to personal relationships. Tell a friend how you really feel about their tendency to interrupt your conversation, chew with their mouth open and forgo the use of deodorant, and you may be rewarded with more, rather than less of that behavior.

Researchers believe this "backfire effect" happens because feedback can often challenge someone's self-perception. This then leads to them defending themselves through unconsciously doubling down on behaviors that may not be serving them, you or the Tribe.

The way around this seems to be asking questions. Rather than stating outright what you feel is the issue, questioning can be used as a subtle, gentler form of feedback.

You may inquire, "Did you see the way that person reacted? Do you think they could have been annoyed by the interruption?" Or "Do you smell that? Did one of us not wear deodorant today?"

I am being purposely humorous, of course, but getting people to observe their own behavior rather than pointing it out to them, has a much better chance of success. This is a strategy all good life coaches employ, and one I use in my life coaching practice all the time. I could tell the person exactly what I see, and sometimes I do, but it is far more powerful when I can help them see it themselves through interested and compassionate questioning.

Here are some other considerations when engaging in conversations with Tribe members or potential Tribe members:

Don't manage emotions
Never try to control someone else's feelings. Speak your truth and recognize that may have consequences. Don't expect them

to take on your emotions or perspective, and don't take on theirs.

Speak from honesty and compassion
Honesty without compassion is cruelty. Strive never to be cruel. Do this by expressing compassion and empathy whenever possible. If someone takes it as harsh, at least you know you did your best to convey understanding.

Try to be open with your shortcomings
You are not perfect and just because you have an opinion does not mean you are right. If possible, admit where you too might be dysfunctional. This also opens the other person up to be more honest and vulnerable.

Responsibility for your Part

All relationships are two-way streets. If there is an issue in a relationship, you are part of it. We teach people how to treat us through our actions so, at the very least, the things that are happening to you are something you have allowed. Do your best to own-up to your part. Of course, it goes without saying that physical, emotional, or verbal abuse is a special circumstance. But even with that, it is almost always under your control to remove yourself from the situation.

Are you open to feedback from others? Make it a point to say, "Look, I have some feelings about this. I could be wrong, but if you are open to some feedback, I will tell you how I feel about it." People generally want, and truly need, feedback from others. This does not mean they won't get angry or have a reaction to your feedback, of course, but asking first increases the likelihood of open, honest communication and lessens the risk for the feedback-giver.

Self-Awareness: Vetting Yourself and Others

I am ordering a coffee at a local coffee shop. It's around the holidays and I am back in the small, southern town I grew up in. A woman walks in and says to another woman standing in line behind me, "Hey sugar! How arrrrrrre you?"

Southerners like to draw out their words like that, and they love to use words like sugar, honey, and darling (daaarlin' if you are trying to say it with a Southern accent).

I smile to myself. I bet that these two ladies barely know one another, and they are just as likely to be talking shit about each other at this week's Christmas parties.

I am next in line, and the young twenty-something barista, who seems offended by my general presence, gives me an annoyed, "What-the-fuck-do-you-want look." She does not ask me what I want, but just looks at me like I am the bane of her existence. She perfectly personifies the name of the coffee shop, *Krankie's*. I get the point and quickly order my coffee.

I smile to myself at this as well. This I understand. This, I think, is genuine. I would not want to be up this early serving people coffee either.

I am a student of psychology and love observing people. I am also human and quick to judge.

I realize how quickly my own biases and stories shaded this interaction. I stop and reflect. I ask myself, "Jade, how do you know that lady is not a genuine sweetheart rather than a bullshitting gossip?" The answer is, I don't.

"How come you reacted more negatively to the pleasant woman compared to the annoyed barista?" The answer is, I don't know.

In the time it takes me to get my coffee and sit down, I have decided who the real asshole is—me.

My history in dealing with Southerners tells me they are often pleasant, but not genuine. They are gossips. My experience living in bigger cities like New York City, Los Angeles and Seattle make me not only tolerant, but understanding, of more authentic people, even if they are rude.

The truth, of course, is I have no idea who these people are in the coffee shop, and I have just made a massive leap of assumptions based on my narrow life experience. Some of my favorite, most genuine people in the world are from the South. Some of the biggest bullshitting, lying assholes I have ever encountered are from the cities I just mentioned. And, when I think about it more deeply, I prefer kind Southerners over rude Northerners any day of the week.

Most of the time...

I know, it's confusing, right? And, given you are human, you likely have the same contradictory reactions regarding people.

10 Ways to Assess Potential Tribe Members

The question you should be asking is, "How do I avoid these types of snap judgments? And, at the same time, how do I not be a pushover?"

Part of the reason we naturally have these types of reactions is that there are bullshitting, lying assholes in the world. Sometimes we are the assholes, and sometimes, someone else is.

The trick is to vet yourself and the individuals you come in contact with. I have several strategies you may want to consider in this regard. Here are my go-to questions for evaluating people in my life, and checking my own asshole tendencies:

What is their history?
This one is tricky because people change. Part of the difficulty

many people have with family and old friends is insisting on seeing them as they were, instead of who they currently are. Still, history matters. If they have been a lying, cheating bullshitter in the past, you might want to keep a closer eye on them. Divorce? Lots of broken friendships? Family drama? I realize I am calling myself out here as well, but the fact remains, history does tell you something. It can't be ignored, but if a person has changed for the better, that is a great sign they can grow, have lessons to teach, and are a potential for your Next Level Tribe.

How do others talk about them?
What do other people say? Do they sing their praises? I have one close friend who I have never heard anyone say anything negative about. In fact, they all say the same thing: "Oh my God, Jane is the sweetest person in the world! I just love her." I have another friend who receives comments that are not as friendly. I have had to defend her when she was not there on a few occasions. Most people who know me well, know I do not tolerate anyone Talking Shit about a friend of mine. Still, there is a stark difference in the way these two are talked about, and I do notice the difference.

How do they talk about others?
This to me says more than most anything else. As we know, there are three types of gossip: Chatting, Dishing and Talking Shit. People who Chat, I don't mind. People who Dish, I am suspicious of, and keep my distance from. People who Shit Talk, I avoid and will engage with as little as possible. We have covered gossip in detail but there are a few other distinctions to which I pay attention.

How does the person respond to a mutual friend's success?

Are they more critical or genuinely excited? How will they behave if another person is talking negatively about someone you
know they consider a friend? Do they defend their friend, or do
they remain quiet? What kind of attitude do they take toward
someone who has made a mistake? Do they say, "Look, we are
all doing the best we can. They made a mistake and I feel badly
for them?' Or are they quick to judge and throw someone else
under the bus?

All of these things matter to me. People are always telling
us exactly who they are if we pay attention. I once had a very
close friend, who I trusted and saw as one of the best people I
knew. One day we were talking about our respective spouses.
Something had gone down in her family, and her husband obviously did not handle it the way she would have liked. Then she
said, "My husband is such a pussy." I remember this literally
jolted me. I could never say anything like that about my wife,
even with our difficulties. Later I would learn that this statement
telegraphed a lot about this person. She had multiple affairs, left
her husband, and ended up with a lot of broken relationships.

Ever since, I have paid close attention to these types of things.
They frequently, but not always, say something very important
about the person. We all go Base Level at times, but when someone does it with the people who are closest to them, I take that
as a sign that person may not be such a great individual.

Do they take responsibility?
As I mentioned in an earlier section, there are two types of
people in the world. If you tell them, "I apologize for my part
in this matter," one type of person will say, "I am very sorry
too. I also had a role to play." The other type of person will say
"Yeah, well you should be" or maybe they will say nothing at all.

If you tell these same people, "Thank you so much, I could not have done it without you," one will say, "Don't be ridiculous, of course, you could have. I am just happy to help." The other may say, "Yeah, good thing I could help." See the difference?

The first type of person displays awareness, consideration, humility, and generosity. The second person demonstrates the opposite of these behaviors. When I first became an entrepreneur, I made it a habit of telling the people who were helping that "I could not be doing it without them." As a result, I had a few of these people start believing exactly that.

The truth was, of course I could do it without them, and actually was.

I said that to express gratitude for their involvement, but it was not actually the truth. This was an example of me wanting to people please versus being authentic and honest. I learned over time that some people immediately seize on things like this, and believe them. Others understand it for what it was, an expression of gratitude. Today I am far more honest and measured in whom, and how, I shower praise on or give credit to. I also pay very close attention to those who take undue credit for things, and those who accept praise with humility and are honest about their actual contributions. This is a self-awareness attribute and it is a critical distinguishing factor I use when looking for Next Level Tribe members.

How do they talk about politics?

Many people insist you should not talk about politics in mixed company, but it is my favorite way to vet people I may want in my Tribe. You may think I am looking for someone who aligns with my political team. Instead, I am looking for a person who does not align with a political affiliation at all. If they jump on a team, it tells me something. If they focus on a single issue, it tells me something. If they remain quiet because they want to "get along," it says something. If they watch only Fox or MSNBC and use team-talk terms like "fake news," "liberal media" or "all conservatives are dumb," it tells me they don't think for themselves.

Watching someone engage in political discussions tells me almost everything I need to know about them. A Next Level Tribe is one committed to growth and learning. Rigid adherence to team dynamics is the opposite of this. Political discussions can tell you so much about a person. Are they ok with disagreements? Do they listen or talk over people? Do they repeat the team talking points or have independent thoughts of their own?

During Donald Trump's run for office, I had several friends who were self-proclaimed "family-values Christians." In response to the constant lies, cruel, and disparaging comments Trump made, I saw two camps emerge. Neither camp was going to vote for Hilary Clinton, but one camp refused to vote for Trump as well. They simply wrote someone else in on the ballot. The other camp went ahead and voted for Trump anyway, justifying his behavior and rationalizing his lies. I have seen this type of behavior on the left and the right, and I find it extremely telling. To me, it means something. It is Culture Level team think and not Next Level behavior.

What are their driving skills like?
Do they let other drivers merge? Do they tailgate? Are they unaware and cut people off? Do they act as if everyone else is stupid and they are the only ones who know how to drive? Do they get anxious and angry in traffic? Do they backseat drive? Are they oblivious to other drivers and asleep at the wheel? All of

these things tell me about their tendency toward consideration, awareness, patience, and control.

Driving is one of those tasks that is a completely unconscious for most people. Our cars have a strange way of making our true behaviors emerge. There are all kinds of things that driving tests. Is the person a rule breaker; running red lights, not completely stopping at stop signs, and/or driving under the influence? The road is a dangerous place and stays safe, partly by all of us agreeing to abide by the rules. This can provide important insight into the person.

I once had a friend who would get irate when someone tried to merge in front of him during times of heavy traffic. He would even pull partially into the fast traffic lane to block them from getting ahead, or he would close the gap between himself and the car in front of him. I was in the car with this friend once when his behavior almost caused an accident. Out of the car he seemed friendly, but again became extremely competitive and judgmental whenever he encountered any type of stress. This person is no longer a member of my friend circle, largely due to this type of behavior.

How do they treat service workers and people on the computer and phone?

How do they treat wait staff, valet attendants, bellman, flight attendants & baristas? How about the homeless, or those asking for handouts? How do they behave in long lines at the bank or coffee shop? Is it all about them? Or do they notice those around them? Do they treat people as equals, or as if they are above them? This tells me about kindness, humility, generosity, and humanity.

This one also rolls over into customer support. It is funny

how being behind a computer screen or telephone can bring out people's true nature. A healthcare provider, who worked with me, once contacted the customer support of my fitness company. She was so incredibly rude to my customer support agents I was seriously taken aback. This person was not well liked, but I had never had any real issues with her. When I saw the language and vitriol she used towards my customer support team, I immediately saw what everyone else was reacting to.

Likewise, the way people comment and what they post on social media is very telling as well. I have a few acquaintances, "friends" on social media, who will post things that tell me a lot about them. During the birther controversy of President Obama's run for office, one person posted an article saying he was the Antichrist. Another one of my friends re-posted the Headless Trump photo that caused controversy shortly after Trump's election. These same people will get in nasty arguments online, and behave in a way that is completely distasteful and off-putting. This stuff matters to me, and I notice. It tells me about their objectivity, decency, integrity, morality and intellectual honesty.

How do they argue?

How do they behave during disagreements? Do they hold a grudge? Do they make the first effort to reconnect and apologize or is it always on you? Are they always right, and you're always wrong? Do you ever hear them say, "I am sorry, I was wrong, and I understand your side"? Can you be in the weeds with them, yell and scream, and then have them come back to talk, apologize and reconnect? This tells you about self-awareness. This tells you about respect. It lets you know they care, and it lets you know they can meet you halfway.

Are they honest? Loyal? Do they have integrity?
Do they blow smoke? Do they avoid? Do their words match their actions? Isn't it funny how all of us hate to be lied to, yet so many of us do it to others? Can you trust the person to be straight with you? More importantly, can you trust them enough to be straight with them? Are they able to be honest and compassionate at the same time? Do they mean what they say, say what they mean and do what they say? This tells you about integrity, honesty, and loyalty.

After I went through my affair, I made a commitment to radical and complete honesty. My friends and family now often comment I am the most honest person they know. I have two intentions in this regard. For my friends, my intention is that they will never have to wonder how I feel about them. I usually volunteer my opinions and views. If my friends want to know something, they need only ask. What I have to say is not always pleasant, but it is always true.

As it pertains to my romantic partners, once I am in a relationship I have an open phone policy. My intention is that they would never be surprised by anything they find on my phone or computer: Anyone I am friends with, they will know about, and be involved with, if they choose. This especially includes my friends of the opposite sex, particularly exes. I don't expect them to be the same way with me, but shady behavior often tells you the person is shady themselves.

How well do they communicate?
This is the number one behavior to assess in people. Good communication requires self-awareness, self-confidence, and self-respect. It is the quintessential skill of all relationships. Do they talk? Talking, even if it is yelling, is always better than silence

or withdrawal. Even the closest of romances and friendships dissolve in the face of non-communication. Do they tell you how they feel, even if they are still unsure about it? Do they include you in their thought process? Is it necessary to them that you have all the information and are not left in the dark? Do they answer your questions? Do they make you feel comfortable sharing your thoughts as well?

After I went through my affair and divorce, I had to take a long hard look at myself and who I was. I did not like who I saw in the mirror. I made a commitment at that time. I said to myself, "From now on I will have no secrets. If I call you a friend, you will never have to wonder how I feel about you or if there is anything I am hiding from you." I committed to honesty, and honesty means communication. Some of the changes I made were to ask people if they wanted to hear my complete thoughts. I started having very tough conversations. I turned on my read receipts on my phone, so everyone knew when I got their text whether I replied to them or not. In a matter of years, I went from someone who was a liar, a cheat and a bull-shitter to someone my friends call one of the most honest people, and best communicators they have ever met. It was not hard to do. I simply decided to own exactly who I was and communicate exactly how I felt when asked.

Final Thoughts

These 10 ways are what I use to assess and vet the people in my life. More importantly, these are the ways I assess myself. To me, self-awareness is the skill that comes before all others. I can never hope to be accurate in my assessment of another if I do not evaluate, and continue to evaluate, my own behavior.

In the end, it is about you. If you see the same patterns

repeating over and over again, it is you. If this person is the only one you have difficulty with, it is likely them.

If you find yourself calling everyone an asshole, you are likely the asshole. If you are reluctant to call anyone an asshole ever, then you may be right in your assessment of the one you think might be.

The point is, judge yourself first. After you have done that, you can use the 10 principles above to evaluate others and vet potential members of your own Next Level Tribe.

Conclusion

• • •

By Jade Teta & Danny Coleman

*"The key is to keep company only with people who
uplift you, whose presence calls forth your best."*
—Epictetus—

Here's to your Next Level Self

As we bring this book to a close, we want you to think about
your hurt for a minute. You are human, so we know you have
pain. We also know those wounds likely include other people.

That pain is most often a result of two things: either you are
unable to connect with new people and feel lonely as a result,
or you have had losses or rejections from those you would like
to be close to.

These types of wounds can last a lifetime. They can also
hinder your ability to develop a supportive Tribe that will help
elevate you to your Next Level Self.

This book is about helping you realize that social connection is a learnable skill. You are responsible for mastering that

skill. You are also accountable for reengaging and recruiting a Tribe that can support you in your growth. Only you can manage your Tribal Battery and own your social behaviors.

Relationships involve learning and growing. If we are your close friends, we should provide both comfort and challenge. We should offer a safe, supportive place for you. We should also inspire, teach, motivate and get you out of your comfort zone so you can grow.

We want to share a philosophy of ours that evolved over time as we coached different individuals. What we noticed is that each of us as human beings are stuck in patterns. We became wrapped up in certain memories and particular stories from our mental autobiographies and have a difficult time seeing past them. In East Indian thought they call this tendency towards getting stuck in stories, *maya*. It means "illusion."

If you analyze these stories and view them in a broader context, you often notice that your life circumstances and past experiences seem eerily suited to help you grow past your old identity and elevate to your Next Level Self.

We noticed that many times our clients were blind to this truth. We could see it, but they could not. Instead, they become convinced the circumstances are the opposite. They see the tough stuff in life as obstacles to progress, rather than opportunities to grow.

Our job as coaches is to help them see the truth.

That truth is this:

Every person that crosses your path provides an opportunity for you to learn and grow. Every problematic situation, conversation, circumstance, and relationship has embedded within it the exact tools required for you to reach your Next Level Self.

You can use what is available to you and choose to do

something with your life. You get to define it. Why are you here? Why did the events in your life happen? What can you make of it? How can you use it?

It's NOT "everything happens for a reason." It's, "things happen and you make a reason."

What if the patterns you have been stuck in since the time you were a child were there to prepare you for the rest of your life? What if those people and circumstances were there to help you realize something you could not understand otherwise? If you started viewing your life from this perspective, would it make a difference? If you started seeing the people in your life this way, would it change things?

I (Jade) had a client, who went through a devastating divorce and betrayal by her husband. She had the rug pulled out from under her feet. She had a life-long fear of abandonment. It was something she had been dealing with since she was a child when her father left. He had a secret, other family.

She developed a complicated relationship with men as a result. The patterns she developed left her with unique challenges in her romantic relationships. The atomic-bomb explosion of being betrayed by her husband forced her to confront what she never had before. That made all the difference for her, and the world. She went to work using the experience to grow. She saw potential and decided to use it.

Rather than continuing to complain about the rug, the person who pulled it, or the wounds sustained in the fall, she turned her attention to the opportunity the fall provided.

She did the work and learned her strength. She escaped from the illusion that she needed a man to care for her. She also developed the power to let any man that did not love and support her go.

She discovered there were people right in front of her that she could grow from. She realized she had to connect with others. She had to trust them, love them, and set boundaries for them, to help cultivate a supportive team and environment. She created a new Tribe.

Not only that, but after her "fall," she realized others had fallen too. She now had the tools to help them get back up and started helping other women make the transition from married to single in middle age.

It did not matter that she did not have a background in counseling. All that mattered is she knew how to be a Counselor, a Coach, a Believer and Tribe member.

She developed experience and wisdom few counselors could provide. Not only did she become a Counselor for her friends, she went back to school and became a qualified counselor and started a new career. She decided that would be her meaning and it made all the difference for her and those women.

Meaning in life is not found. You don't find it in a job. It does not manifest in some nonsensical, "you complete me" romantic connection. Your kids can provide a temporary meaning, but in the end, you need to find your own—kids grow up after all.

Meaning comes from using your signature strengths to impact positive change in the world. Real meaning is rarely about just you. Meaning comes from sharing your gifts with your social connections.

You have a unique set of gifts, experiences, and wisdom that only you can bring to the world. Those same gifts are needed desperately by others who may be struggling in those areas. For some, yours is the only voice they will be able to hear.

You matter more than you know. Your work and your energy are important.

Your Next Level Self must be revealed. Being a Next Level Friend and creating a Next Level Tribe are both essential for your growth.

Without your higher self in the world, people suffer more than necessary. For example, let's say your father passed away from a very long and painful sickness. You sharing the lessons from your father's illness can help another person make sense of the loss of their family member. They are healed more completely from you telling your story. When you realize the impact you can make by sharing your lessons, you give your pain a purpose. It is a feed forward, mutually beneficial dynamic. With your Next Level Self, the world is aided in ways it could never be otherwise. People are enhanced in ways you can't imagine or even fully understand. Your Tribal Battery is charged and sustained as well.

Your life and your social circle are important. The happier and more connected you are, the more you can bring to the world. This is why you must find your Next Level Tribe and become your Next Level Self. We hope this book has helped in some small way.

To your Next Level!
Jade and Danny
2018

Made in the USA
San Bernardino, CA
07 December 2018